Popular Culture in the Classroom

Teaching and Researching Critical Media Literacy

Popular Culture in the Classroom

Teaching and Researching Critical Media Literacy

Donna E. Alvermann

Jennifer S. Moon

Margaret C. Hagood

University of Georgia

Athens, Georgia, USA

INTERNATIONAL Reading Association

800 Barksdale Road
PO Box 8139
Newark, Delaware 19714-8139, USA
www.reading.org

National Reading Conference
122 South Michigan Avenue
Suite 1100
Chicago, Illinois 60603, USA

Library of Congress Cataloging in Publication Data
Alvermann, Donna E.
  Popular culture in the classroom: Teaching and researching critical media literacy/Donna E. Alvermann, Jennifer S. Moon, Margaret C. Hagood.
    p.   cm.
  Includes bibliographical references (p.) and index.
  1. Media literacy—Study and teaching.   2. Popular culture—Study and teaching.
I. Moon, Jennifer S.   II. Hagood, Margaret C.   III. Title.
P1.3.A485   1999   98-54821
302.23'07—dc21
ISBN 0-87207-245-2

Contents

Note From the Series Editors

Donna Alvermann, Jennifer Moon, and Margaret Hagood have given us a state-of-the-art look into the world of popular culture. To say that this volume is creative and exciting is only to begin to describe this provocative work. It will capture its readers' imaginations with its poignantly presented anecdotes about the role of popular culture in children's and adolescents' lives. Its subtle, yet insightful, treatment of U.S. popular culture is a treat for all readers. The authors trace the roots of popular culture in the United States, vividly contrasting them with other forms of culture including folk culture, mass culture, and youth culture. This fascinating book answers many of our unformed questions and is years ahead of its time. We believe it will become a landmark text that will influence all educators who serve the literacy needs of children and adolescents.

We hope that this excellent volume will serve as a reference tool as educators plan literacy programs for learners of all ages and cultures. This book as well as others in the Literacy Studies Series broadens our understanding of research and provides guidance as instructional practices are designed. The goal of the Series is to advance knowledge in the literacy field and to help make research a more important focus in the literacy community. The volumes in this Series are intended to inform literacy instruction and research by reporting findings from state-of-the-art literacy endeavors. We believe that this text successfully accomplishes this goal.

James Flood
Diane Lapp
Series Editors
San Diego State University
San Diego, California, USA

Review Board

ix

Dr. Nancy C. Padak
Kent State University
Kent, Ohio

Dr. Jeanne R. Paratore
Boston University
Boston, Massachusetts

Dr. Victoria Purcell-Gates
Harvard University
Cambridge, Massachusetts

Dr. Nancy L. Roser
University of Texas at Austin
Austin, Texas

Dr. Diane L. Schallert
University of Texas at Austin
Austin, Texas

Dr. Lyndon W. Searfoss
Arizona State University
Tucson, Arizona

Dr. Peter N. Winograd
University of New Mexico
Albuquerque, New Mexico

Dr. M. Jo Worthy
University of Texas at Austin
Austin, Texas

Foreword

It is New Year's Day, 1999, as I write this foreword. Last year was the year of the newly "spiritual" Madonna, the manufactured "girl power" of the Spice Girls, the "postfeminism" of Ally McBeal, and the market success of *Titanic*'s Rose. These popular symbols, and others like them, are the texts that figure most prominently in many students' lives, in the United States and globally. And as Donna Alvermann, Jennifer Moon, and Margaret Hagood make clear, these are texts that students interpret and reinterpret, embrace and contest, discuss and emulate on a daily basis. Thus, *Popular Culture in the Classroom: Teaching and Researching Critical Media Literacy* is a timely and important addition to the field of literacy education and to the Literacy Studies Series. This book fills a void in our field, and it does so with great acumen.

Demonstrating the praxis of teaching and researching critical media literacy is a central goal of this book, a goal that is singularly achieved. The connection between theory and practice is especially important to this book's success because many readers will be introduced here, for the first time, to theories related to critical media and popular culture studies. These fields are themselves interdisciplinary, drawing as they do from cultural studies, feminist studies, and critical theory. Yet the authors manage to explain theoretical perspectives so that they are accessible and usable to readers. Literacy teachers and researchers, often most at home with print texts, are introduced here to ways of reading and responding to nonprint texts and other symbolic forms, as well as strategies for teaching such texts and forms.

This is a book that examines the significance of youth cultures as they intersect with classroom life. How do young people use resources from popular culture to challenge or change authoritative cultural norms? How might literacy educators and researchers determine when to promote the critical analysis of popular culture? What does it mean to derive pleasure from popular culture in the face of its market-driven interests and their gender, race, and class biases? These are some of the difficult questions addressed in this volume.

Current interest in student-centered classrooms that allow for student choice underscores the need for critical media education. Student-centered pedagogies empower students to bring to the classroom cultural materials and resources that teachers often do not feel comfortable legitimating. Yet, as the authors of this book point out, to prohibit references to popular culture in the classroom can serve to increase its subcultural value among students. Educators and researchers must become critical consumers and teachers of the media, this book argues; yet the book also points to certain contradictions: the way that age distances us from youth cultures as they have been shaped by the popular media; the difficulty of teaching a subject about which students are the experts; and the ephemeral quality of cultural symbols that change or disappear just as we begin to learn about them.

This book invites us to consider a variety of approaches to critical media studies in the classroom. We join the authors as each takes us into a particular classroom where she teaches a lesson that includes some media symbol or popular form. In the process, we learn of each author's uncertainties and revisions, her questions and epiphanies. The authors are very present in this volume, despite its strong theoretical component and its thorough review of research. They invite us to consider four possible approaches to teaching critical media literacy, highlighting the benefits and drawbacks of each approach. In the end, they argue for a "self-reflexive" approach that respects the pleasure students take from popular culture while helping students examine the political economy of popular consumption.

Alvermann, Moon, and Hagood make a convincing argument for those of us who research and teach literacy to take up the call for critical media literacy. Not to do so is to miss the opportunity to engage students in examining the kind of culture that increasingly shapes their lives and ours.

Cynthia Lewis
University of Iowa
Iowa City, Iowa, USA

Acknowledgments

Writing a book for the IRA/NRC Literacy Studies Series has been a highlight of our collaboration as coauthors. And, because like most work of this nature the collaboration involved more people than ourselves, we would like to acknowledge a number of individuals who figured prominently in the book's origination and final production.

We are especially indebted to James Flood and Diane Lapp, who as coeditors of the Series thought our proposal for a book on the intersection of critical media literacy and popular culture was a good idea; to Allan Luke, whose advice at a critical point in the book's development led to a major change in direction; to the students and their teachers, whose invitation to work in their classroom allowed us to put theory into practice; and to our anonymous reviewers, whose comments and suggestions helped to shape the book (and our thinking, in the process).

For the patience, skill, and good humor that went into preparing the manuscript, we are indebted to Jennifer Guyton, DeAnna Palmer, and Suzette Whitehead. Finally, we thank Matt Baker, whose expertise in guiding this book through to production made the project an enjoyable one to the very end.

CHAPTER 1

Teaching Critical Media Literacy Using Popular Culture Texts

Popular Culture in the Classroom: Teaching and Researching Critical Media Literacy is a book written for teachers, researchers, and theorists who have grown up in a world radically different from that of the students they teach, study, and theorize about. Carmen Luke (1997) wrote that there is an "urgent need for educators to engage constructively with media, popular and youth culture to better understand how these discourses structure childhood, adolescence, and students' knowledge" (p. 45). As literacy educators, we believe there is a special need to understand how cultural and political contexts influence the questions that teachers and researchers ask about popular media texts (for example, who produces these texts, for what purposes, and for whose consumption). It is toward such understandings that we developed this book.

What Is Critical Media Literacy?

The term *critical media literacy*, a concept best defined by taking into account some of the work being done in sociology and the interdisciplinary area known as cultural studies, has to do with providing individuals access to understanding how the print and nonprint texts that are part of everyday life help to construct their knowledge of the world and the various social, economic, and political positions they occupy within it (Baker & Luke, 1991; Christian-Smith, 1997; Luke, 1997). Critical media literacy is also about creating communities of active readers and writers who can be expected to exercise some degree of agency in deciding what textual positions they will assume or resist as they interact in complex social and cultural contexts (Buckingham, 1998; Hilton, 1996; Luke, 1998).

This conception of critical media literacy follows up on what Allan Luke and Peter Freebody (1997b) have referred to as the move away from psychological and personal growth models of reading toward the view that reading is a social and cultural practice. In their words,

> This move is significant in terms of how we see difference and diversity in the classroom.... In so far as we view literacy as a psychological phenomenon, we will tend to define classroom problems in terms of student lack.... Instead, a sociological approach focuses on the kinds of discourses, language, and practices that students have had access to and practice with. These are the products of participation and membership in particular interpretive communities, not of simple individual difference. They are the resources of cultural practice, not of innate intelligence, natural ability, or developmental stages. (p. 208)

Finally, it is important to consider that our conceptions of critical media literacy do not deny the psychological or cognitive aspects of reading, writing, and speaking; instead, we see them as attendant processes in a much larger social context—one in which "literacy is always already political" (Green, 1997, p. 241) and relations of power are at stake in people's daily interactions around popular culture forms. We also acknowledge that issues of gender, race, class, age, and other identity markers are historically part of these everyday interactions (Luke & Freebody, 1997a).

Living in an Age of Popular Culture

We are living in an age often portrayed as being dominated by consumer capitalism and the products of a capitalistic mass culture—for example, shopping malls, tabloid newspapers, talk shows, Music Television (MTV), and the World Wide Web. Consumers of all ages and backgrounds, but children and youth in particular, often are criticized for mindlessly buying into these cultural artifacts. Popular consumption of cultural phenomena such as computer games, MTV, chat rooms on the Internet, video arcades, comics, Madonna, and the television shows *South Park* and *Ally McBeal* produces texts of a sort, which in turn evoke different responses from different people. For example, popular culture theorist John Fiske (1989a) has pointed out that for some audiences Madonna is read as nothing more than a "boy toy" while for others she personifies a resistance to patriarchy's definition of what a woman should be, do, and say.

This oppositional reading of a text, in the broad sense of the term, is what Fiske (1989b) sees as the distinguishing characteristic between mass culture and popular culture. Refusing to equate mass culture with popular culture, Fiske has argued that mass culture represents the goods with which a capitalistic society attempts to dominate and homogenize people's thinking, whereas popular culture reflects people's bid to evade and manipulate those attempts, such as when Madonna assumes the image of "The Material Girl." To Fiske, it is this manipulative aspect of popular culture that enables subordinated groups (for example, women, children, and minorities) to subvert mass culture's attempts to dominate their lives by telling them through the media's influence what they should be, do, and say. He also believes that an audience's ability to oppose or resist the media's influence is more or less a "natural" response—not a practice that needs to be taught formally.

Although she agrees that children are not dupes of the media that some adults may make them out to be, Carmen Luke (1997) is not content to sit back and wait for children to develop the subversive practices Fiske (1989a, 1989b) has outlined. Instead, she has argued for developing a critical awareness of the media that begins as early as the primary grades and extends through teacher education programs at the graduate level. Luke has cautioned, however, that teachers should not insist that students learn to critique the very texts (film, video, print) in which they take pleasure. She wrote the following:

> By asking children in the public forum of the classroom to undertake...[a] critique of the texts that are important to them and that usually form a subversive counterpoint to the discourse of schooling, teachers unwittingly position students to reveal and possibly disavow their "secret pleasures." In other words, by giving students the technical skills with which to dismantle and dismiss ideologically incorrect texts—to

3

identify stereotyping, class bias, sexist or racist content—we ask them to expose and confess to desires, and publicly to confess their dislike of [television] programs that they probably like a lot. (p. 43)

Murdock (1997), who writes widely on contemporary culture and communication, also sees a problem in counting on children and adolescents to engage in the subversive practice of "doing popular culture" (cf. West & Zimmerman, 1987, on doing gender) as a way of resisting mass media's messages. For Murdock, there is a danger in romanticizing or celebrating the consumer's right to refuse these messages. For example, what if a child repeatedly fails to exercise this right and adopts wholesale the images offered by the dominant forces of consumer capitalism? Moreover, Murdock sees in Fiske's (1989b) stance the potential for colluding (however unwittingly) with the neoconservative view of the world as a marketplace where concerns about individual freedoms should take precedence over concerns about the common good.

Why a Book on Teaching Critical Media Literacy?

Perhaps at no other time in the history of literacy education have more demands been put on teachers to develop within students an ability to read and critique a wide range of media texts. A small but growing body of research on critical media literacy (for example, Dyson, 1997; Finders, 1996; Lewis, 1997; Luke, 1997; Neilsen, 1998) points to the importance of developing within children and adolescents a critical awareness of the social, political, and economic messages emanating from popular fiction, music, movies, comics, magazines, videos, computer games, and other popular culture forms.

The ability to read and critique popular media is significant for at least two reasons. First, in an age of expanding consumerism, children and young people who learn to question how their identities are constructed by the various forms of popular culture that they elect to take up are likely to make more informed decisions about how they live their lives. Second, the abundance of media messages (both image based and verbal) in the home and community suggests that there is an urgent need to help students learn how to evaluate such messages for their social, political, economic, and aesthetic contents.

4

Organization of the Book

This chapter introduces what we mean by critical media literacy and the different interests and cultural resources each author brings to the book. It also lays out a rationale for teaching critical media literacy using popular culture texts and offers four scenarios designed to engage readers in experiencing some of those texts. Chapter 2 considers issues surrounding the selection and introduction of popular culture texts for use in critical media literacy lessons, then offers some cautionary notes to teachers about the politics of pleasure, that is, to the potential conflict between students' desires and what they know is "politically correct" to say or do. It also addresses what it means to be part of an audience and the role of the teacher in relation to both pleasure and audience. Chapters 3, 4, and 5 provide examples of teaching strategies that we have used at the primary, upper elementary, and middle school levels to engage students in critical media literacy lessons. Artifacts from these lessons also are included along with self-reflections on what we learned from working with popular culture texts in regular classroom settings. Chapter 6 gives a detailed analysis of how children's and adolescents' identities are constructed through the media in an age of popular culture. The chapter argues against a monolithic view of either youth or the media's representation of popular culture and gives special attention to how readers take up or resist the textual positionings available to them through the media. Chapter 7 synthesizes and explores where the literacy field is and needs to go in theorizing and researching critical media literacy. We chose to address theory and research last in order to draw from previous chapters those issues that seemed most relevant as we reflected on our own initiation as teachers and researchers of critical media literacy in an age of popular culture.

The Stories Behind Our Interest in Writing This Book

As authors, each of us brings different interests, experiences, and interpretations of those experiences to our teaching, researching, and writing. In the sections that follow, we tell our own stories (hence, the use of "I" instead of "we") about various background experiences that led us to write this book.

Donna's Story

How did I become interested in teaching critical media literacy using popular culture, not to mention writing a book on the topic? In terms of background, I have been reading and conducting research on how gender intersects with literacy teaching and learning (an aspect of critical literacy) for a little over 6 years. However, my knowledge of the literature on popular culture was very limited before I began work on this book. Apart from having seen a few episodes of *The Simpsons* and *Beavis and Butthead*, I knew very little about contemporary media. I had attended R.E.M.'s benefit concert for the Clinton/Gore U.S. presidential team a few years ago when Vice President Gore came to Athens, Georgia, and I do read *The New York Times* Arts and Leisure section on a regular basis. Occasionally, I scan *Newsweek*'s cyberscope department, but I have not found or taken the time to venture far on the World Wide Web—at least not into the chat rooms where the latest popular culture phenomenon is sure to be discussed at length.

All this changed, however, when I began experimenting with some critical media literacy activities in my graduate-level content area reading class for preservice and inservice teachers, grades 1–12. Soon, two of the students in the class began putting videotaped copies of the newest television hit *South Park* in my office mailbox along with newspaper clippings about this low-budget cartoon's "raucously subversive look at small-town life in all its complexities" (Robinson, 1998, p. 25). Other students, mostly women in their mid- to late-20s, let me know how much they enjoyed learning a particular content area reading strategy that I had introduced by juxtaposing two critical reviews of the *Ally McBeal* show on Fox television. Another student in the class (a woman who had participated minimally in discussions previous to the Ally McBeal activity) e-mailed me that she was surprised but pleased to see I had taken the risks she associated with using popular culture in an academic setting. Out of 25 students (predominantly white women), only one had negative comments to report on the course evaluation form regarding my use of the Ally McBeal texts.

As word spread of my interest in writing a book on critical media literacy using popular culture texts, information started arriving in the mail, over e-mail, and by word of mouth. For example, I received a package from Carmen Luke in Australia that contained a number of articles on contemporary media literacy, including a critique of several advertisements for cyberculture software. Friends began e-mailing me Web site addresses to check out, and some even sent me copies of newsletters that listed these sites in hard-copy form. Colleagues dropped off issues of recent newspapers and magazines that featured the latest articles on new forms of music such as "popabilly hip-hop" and reviews of a controversial movie rumored not to be shown in any local theaters. Soon, I discovered that my fairly meager knowledge about popular culture was increasing exponentially. In true rhizome fashion (Deleuze & Guattari, 1987), offshoots from one information source spread to other sources, sometimes fragmenting into unregulated networks that took off on their own.

Jennifer's Story

As children growing up in New York City, the first thing my brother, sister, and I would do daily after arriving home from school was to turn on the television. Both of our parents worked and would not be home for hours, and because we were told to stay inside and off the streets, our television stayed on until our parents came home. Those several hours after school became a time when my siblings and I were in our own world. Even before the term *channel surfing* became popular, we were already practitioners. We would flip through the channels to watch one show after another with no breaks in between. We went from *Tom and Jerry* to *Fantastic Four* to *The Flintstones* to *The Jetsons* and then to *Gilligan's Island*. On Saturday mornings, we got up along with thousands of other children our age and watched the *X-Men* and the endless stream of cartoons and, in the afternoons, martial arts movies (the type in which the actors' mouths and the dubbed English dialogue never matched).

For us and many other latchkey children who grew up in a city, television became a natural part of our lives that was separate from our school lives. For us, school and the things we did in the privacy of our home (watching television, playing video games, and reading magazines) were separate worlds that did not overlap, except when we had to make arrangements with our parents to do our homework first and then watch television. Even as an adult, and now a doctoral stu-

7

dent, I find myself feeling out of sorts if I do not turn on the television immediately after arriving home at the end of the day. Despite an inner voice that nags me to do my "scholarly reading" rather than watching television, I find myself substituting popular adult television programs—*Friends*, *Seinfeld*, *The X-Files*, *Living Single*, *Ellen*, and *Mad About You*—for my childhood cartoons.

However, even with my voracious television watching, I was unaware of shows such as *Ally McBeal* and *South Park* until I became involved in writing this book. I soon began searching the Internet and leafing through popular magazines, newspapers, and books, and I made sure that I watched *Ally McBeal*. The more informed I became about the media and popular culture, the more complex they became in my mind. In the process of writing this book I have come to appreciate the intriguing questions about how popular culture can impact students, teachers, and researchers.

Margaret's Story

I am a product of the television and computer era. I grew up watching cable television, specifically MTV, and playing Atari video games. As part of my elementary school curriculum, I was taught how to write basic five-line computer programs including the commands "Go To" and "Run" and how to type on a word processor. I was well acquainted with all the characters on *The Partridge Family* and *The Brady Bunch* and scheduled my activities around the times of the programs. I went through phases of wearing miniskirts, reading *The Preppy Handbook*, and making friendship bracelets.

Then everything changed. I went to college and decided to become an educator. During that developmental period of becoming an adult who would influence children in classrooms, I began to think that only scholastic activities and educational entertainment held merit. I recall, at that point in my life, discrediting television that I did not deem educational, snubbing books that were not award winners, and believing that computer games were the downfall of America's children. I remained in this mindset throughout college and my years of elementary school teaching.

While in the classroom I remember discouraging my students from playing with television action figures on the playground, from writing about Walt Disney characters during free-writing activities, and from reading stories from R.L. Stine's Goosebumps series during sustained silent reading. I thought that I was assisting my students' learning by indirectly teaching them that they were more creative and intelligent than these forms of popular culture that I believed lacked educational value.

In the past few months working on this book, I have had to rethink all the beliefs that I have lived by these past several years. As I read and learn more about critical media literacy, I find myself having in-depth conversations with third- and fourth-grade students about their W.W.J.D.? (What Would Jesus Do?) bracelets, reading first graders' creative writing pieces about new Beanie Baby designs, and listening to fifth-grade students debate the fastest way to save the monkey from the dinosaur hunter on a video game. And I have found that, if allowed, students are interested and enthusiastic about sharing their thoughts with adults.

My interest in critical media literacy has come about as a result of being flexible and open to learning about it, learning from it, and learning through it. Observing children engaged in meaningful activities centered around their worlds has forced me to stop and rethink what schooling is about. Allowing children to bring themselves entirely into the educational arena could validate who they are and perhaps increase their genuine interest in reading, writing, and discussing their perspectives of the world while simultaneously allowing them to explore the perspectives of others. I now find myself pondering the unlimited possibilities that critical media literacy could have on children's creativity and on their motivation to initiate participation in classroom literacy activities.

A Rationale for Teaching Critical Media Literacy Using Popular Culture Texts

The act of reading is no longer perceived as transmitting facts from the printed page to the mind. Nor are texts perceived any more as that narrow vein of technology known as print media. Today's reader interprets a broad range of texts that use a variety of symbols, or signs, to communicate their messages. For example, the sign systems employed by musicians, artists (including computer graphic artists), choreographers, dramatists, video technicians, mathematicians, and traditionally oral societies also count as texts—texts that can be read with varying success by readers who are adept at using multiple sign systems, or literacies, to interpret their worlds. The disciplinary field that studies these different sign systems and how they have evolved historically is called *semiotics*, from a Greek word meaning a symbol or sign that has meaning attached to it.

By bringing a semiotic approach to critical media literacy, it is possible to treat all forms of popular culture as *signs*—as a language through which meaning is communicated using words, images, and objects from everyday life. Originally, it was Saussure's (1960) work in linguistics that foreshadowed the study of signs as a means of understanding a society's culture, including the words, images, and objects of popular culture that function as signifiers in the production of meaning about certain concepts (the signifieds). It also was Saussure who broke with the notion that language comes from within people; instead he maintained that as individuals we are dependent on others who share our cultural codes to make language meaningful. And these codes change as witnessed, for example, by the different meanings that words such as *jeans* and *woman* have come to signify since the 1960s. To be literate in today's highly complex and technologically advanced society, it is important to read the signs of our times with a critical awareness that is equally applicable to school-sanctioned texts and those of contemporary culture.

If notions about readers and texts are changing, so, too, are the contexts in which the various sign systems just described are being interpreted. Increasingly, these contexts are the very classroom communities in which we work, whether at the primary, middle school, high school, or college level. Teaching critical media literacy using popular culture texts with groups of students who often know more than we do about current trends in alternative rock music, film making, computer technology, and video software can be challenging. For example, how do we catch up with a world that is moving quickly in many directions and on many fronts? Maintaining the status quo is not an option. As Bertram Bruce (1997), a literacy educator long interested in the transformative nature of technology, would remind us, students (and all people) need the literacy technologies available today if they are to function in society and make use of the information and services currently in existence and those still to come.

To bring Bruce's (1997) message closer to home, consider some anecdotal evidence shared at a preconvention institute sponsored by the International Reading Association on the crises in adolescent literacy. The evidence was gathered by Tom Bean working collaboratively with his two adolescent daughters, Shannon and Kristen (Bean, Bean, & Bean, 1998), in a project designed to find out how various forms of print and nonprint media figured into their lives both in and out of school. Similar to what Finders (1997), Neilsen (1998), and O'Brien (1998) had found in their work with adolescent literacy, Bean reported that Shannon and Kristen used a variety of technologies (novels, textbooks, notes passed to friends, movies, computers, television, and telephone) to engage socially and academically with literacy both in and out of school. Although Bean and his daughters were quick to point out that their results could in no way generalize beyond their household, there is a familiarity in what they found that we think cannot be ignored.

This anecdote leaves the reader with a rich mosaic of how easily and effortlessly students are able to connect print and nonprint media, as well as school and nonschool literacies. As adults we need only listen and be convinced that students' ways of interacting with the world are valuable and at least equally viable in our world. If we take seriously Bakhtin's (1981) work on dialogism that led Cintron (1991) to note the inseparability of youth and adult subgroups in the larger culture, then it is possible that the divide between in-school and out-of-school literacies will be crossed. Certainly, as the contents of this book will suggest, we would be well-served to learn how readers, texts, and contexts construct and are constructed by the media, if for no other reason than to make visible popular culture's invisibility in the classroom.

Popular Culture Texts and Discourse Communities

This section is divided into four scenarios that will introduce you to different kinds of popular culture texts, and just as importantly, to the concept of discourse communities. In each scenario you will be asked to imagine yourself in a situation that calls for action on your part. Knowing which discourse community is informing your response to a particular situation is basic to understanding other concepts, such as positioning and audience, which are introduced here and elaborated on in later chapters.

Because we hold multiple and concurrent memberships in various discourse communities (for example, we may be professionals, parents, sons or daughters, liberals or conservatives) we tend to see things differently according to the discourse "hat" we don. Even within a given discourse community, we are never the unitary subjects we might imagine ourselves to be. Therefore, in each scenario that follows, you should identify the discourse community or communities in which you are claiming membership before choosing the action you will take. Although these scenarios work best when you are part of a group that shares orally, it is possible when working alone to respond in your journal (if you keep one), or simply to reflect on why you have chosen a particular action over another. By reflecting on your choices in this manner, it is likely you will develop a better understanding of the multiple and often conflicting discourse communities of which you are a member.

Scenario One

You are seated in an audience at the 1998 Qualitative Research in Education Conference at the University of Georgia's Continuing Education Center. Lorri Neilsen, one of the presenters in the session you are attending, is giving some background information on a series of interviews she conducted with her 17-year-old son David and his teenage friend Eleanor. Given the session's time constraints, Lorri will be sharing only certain parts from several interviews that address David's and Eleanor's engagement with the world through print and nonprint texts.

First, Lorri gives some background on the interview project she embarked on, partly out of her interest as a teacher educator in how adolescents draw from popular culture texts to create their own social identities. Her comments follow:

> The premise of my [talk] is that engagements with texts in everyday life help all readers and writers to shape their identities (and reshape them, in an ongoing process), and further, that adolescents, in particu-

lar, engage in more fluid, intentional, and often more passionate identity play in their encounters with texts. Whether their "text" is a school-sanctioned reading requirement, a beach novel, a style of dressing, a conversational pattern, or a popular film, texts hold potential as symbolic resources.... These symbolic resources not only help adolescents to make sense of their experiences, but they also offer opportunities for trying on or taking up often multiple and conflicting roles or identities. In this way, a text is both window and door.... Adolescents, who typically demonstrate as much zeal in taking up roles as they do in resisting them, become performers in their own right simultaneously being both actor and theater, performer and audience, in their engagement with the world through texts. By reading and writing the texts of their lives, they are reading and writing themselves. (Neilsen, 1998, p. 4)

The film under discussion in David's comments is Quentin Tarantino's *Pulp Fiction*, which won the Cannes Film Festival's highest prize and an Academy Award for best original screenplay. Despite these honors, the film has been criticized for its graphic violence. David's comments follow:

I liked the way the story was told—the story line all jumbled. I liked the cinematography and the dialogue. It was both vulgar and smart. I liked the way the dialogue got into detail about little things.

I went not because of Travolta, but because everyone was raving about it. It scared me, actually, because of my reaction to the violence. Some of the violent scenes just were nothing, which made me wonder if I was overexposed to violence. They were brutal, but what got to me—when I really freaked out—was when Vincent was putting the needle into Mia's heart. You know, the adrenaline to revive her. I mean he was saving her life, not killing her like all the rest of the violence in the movie, but saving her, and that's the part that really affected me.

And I really liked the way Tarantino messed with linear structure and chopped up the film.... Plus the writing was really good. You know, the dialogue about nothing.... My close friends and I got the sound track...which also added to my love for the film because there were excerpts from the movie on the soundtrack, which I memorized.... We even went so far as to do our own *Pulp Fiction* movie, Simon and I. We took the video camera from Simon's house, decided to look for an old building that looked kind of '70s, carpeted and all that. We found a place on Queen Street, went up to one of the floors and asked Simon's sister to film us. We walked around, we were dressed up, and then we went downstairs and did the scene about Royale with cheese.

Then we did the play at school, which I directed. It intrigued me…. I found the script on the Internet, printed off sections that I wanted. I would have printed off other sections but I couldn't because it was for the school…. I had to be selective. It was too bad, because I had to leave out some of the best scenes…. Ross [another friend of David's] and I still want to put *Pulp Fiction* in its linear order and see what kind of movie it turns out to be.

Quentin Tarantino seems like us. Hanging around making films. Hanging out with friends. Our conversations are like that kind of dialogue. Or like *Seinfeld*. I mean, maybe we're mocking them, but…we joke around with each other…. We argue about nothing and are funny. Like Ross will go, hey, I like your shoes, let's just say. And I go, yeah, man, they are the shoes. And Ross will say, Oh, they *are* the shoes. And then we just go off talking about shoes. Just think of a situation and we'd try to one up each other, playing, not like competition, but to try to come up with better lines. (Neilsen, 1998, pp. 15–18)

Now it is your turn. Decide which of the following actions you would take, and tell why. Be sure to identify the discourse community or communities you represent.

Action 1: Engage David in a more in-depth discussion of why most of the violence in *Pulp Fiction* failed to affect him.

Action 2: Congratulate the teacher who allowed David and his friend, Simon, to produce a version of *Pulp Fiction* for a school audience.

Action 3: Schedule a meeting with the school district's curriculum director to determine if popular culture texts are used widely in the schools and with what effects.

Action 4: Read more about how young people draw from popular culture to construct their own identities.

Action 5: Suggest your own plan of action.

Reflection. Consider for a moment how the response you gave depended on the discourse community you had in mind when you selected one action over another. Did you find yourself torn between choosing one action over another? If so, how might you explain the fact that you are able to cross over from one discourse community to another?

Scenario Two

You have just heard on the evening news that 54% of the parents surveyed in your state say they do not use the rating codes when selecting television programs for family viewing. Another 68% say they do not understand the codes. Then, when changing the channels, your attention is drawn to the fact that the show *South Park* is airing in 1 hour at 10 p.m. You make a mental note to watch tonight's episode. You have been hearing people at work talk about this show, and the cover of the latest issue of *Newsweek* lying on your table has the cartoon faces of Stan, Kyle, Cartman, and Kenny—the four foul-mouthed third graders who are the main characters on the show. Superimposed on the magazine cover are these words:

> South Park!*
> TV's Rude, Crude Comedy Hit
> *(Ask Your Kids)

Inside on the contents page is the following description of the cover:

> THE COVER: A twisted underground cartoon is now a pop-cult obsession. Welcome to "South Park," a paranormal Colorado town inhabited by flatulent third-graders—a grown-up show with irresistible kid appeal. Page 56

You turn to the seven-page feature in the magazine and begin to read. You find that *South Park* is fast turning Wednesday and Saturday nights into family nights. You also learn that a recent ruling by the Federal Communications Commission (FCC) that will enable parents to block the show by buying televisions with FCC approved built-in V-chips, which censor violence and sexually explicit material, may not be necessary. According to the writer of the article (Marin, 1998), already 23% of the viewing audience is under 18, and with 5.2 million cable television viewers, *South Park* (which airs on Comedy Central) recently beat the ABC network's news program *Prime Time Live* in the ratings game. This rings a bell with you, having just recalled seeing an earlier CNN factoid that listed *South Park* as the highest rated cable show outside of sporting events.

After finishing the *South Park* article, you page through the rest of the issue and pause, as usual, at the Newsmakers Department. There, your eye fixates momentarily on this string of words: *popabilly hip-hop hit*. What kind of music, you ask yourself, could the word *popabilly* refer to? Intrigued, you read on and learn that the song "Are You

Jimmy Ray?" is an example of popabilly hip-hop music. You search for clues as to what this genre is about, but all you can gather is what the songwriter (Jimmy Ray) says: "It's fun.... You can sing along. You know, don't bore us, get to the chorus" (Hammer, 1998, p. 47). Finishing this short piece, you discover that "Are You Jimmy Ray?", which is considered the genre's perfect song, is expected to move into *Billboard* magazine's chart of top 10 singles.

Now, decide which of the following actions you will take, and why. Don't forget to name the discourse community or communities of which you are a part.

Action 1: Turn off the television; you have had enough of popular culture for the night.

Action 2: Ask your own children, or the children of your relatives or neighbors, what they know about *South Park* and popabilly hip-hop.

Action 3: Write a response to the *South Park* feature and send it to *Newsweek*'s letters to the editor department.

Action 4: Make a pledge to yourself that you will become better informed about popular culture's texts.

Action 5: Suggest your own plan of action.

Reflection. Reflect now on the content of the articles you just perused. Is it alien to you? What discourse community might find the content interesting? Could you imagine yourself ever becoming part of that discourse community? Why or why not?

Scenario Three

You are shopping for some Internet software at your local discount store. Confused by the many choices available and being somewhat of a novice in this area, you find a salesperson and ask for advice. The person suggests you consider Prodigy's *Amber* and then hands you the advertisement in Figure 1, which shows an adolescent girl with this message typed in quotation marks to one side of the ad: "It all started when I typed hello."

Featured in the March 1996 issue of *Wired*, a magazine for the cyberculture crowd, this advertisement illustrates what Luke and Luke (1997) consider to be the gendered politics of naming. It positions the reader in one or more ways. As you learn what Luke and Luke

Figure 1
Prodigy's *Amber*

"It all
started
when
I typed
hello."

The online experience. It's out there. An undefined space with thousands of people. Chatting, connecting, exchanging ideas. See what you've been missing. Plug into Prodigy. There's never been a better time. We'll give you **10 free hours,* free software and a free trial month** on the New Prodigy. Interested? Then we need to know who you are. You know the drill.

Name

Address

City/State/Zip

We'll send you software for Windows™ 3.1 (or greater) on □CD-ROM or □3.5" disk.
Call 1 800-PRODIGY, ext. 1161.

the new ✪ *prodigy*
whatever you're into

From *Wired*, March 1996. Advertisement for Prodigy Internet.

have to say about this text in the following excerpt, see if you agree or disagree with their analysis:

> "It all started when I typed hello." We can read this to be a take on the way we talk about the start of an intimate relationship which, taking a cue from Amber's winsome smile, might just suggest that "the on-line experience" really did start something more than a chat-group experience. The sexual innuendo here is hard to miss. We note that Amber is in quotation marks which tells us that Amber is her sigfile, her on-line persona.
>
> She leans her hand into her neck which catches some hair strands pushed against her lips. Her smile betrays nothing: can we assume she's just come off-line after a particularly satisfying on-line encounter, or is she

waiting to plug in to get into "whatever you're into," or is she just taking a reflective moment to ruminate over the Prodigy experience? (Luke & Luke, 1997, p. 56)

You finish reading the advertisement and look around for the salesperson, who has disappeared in the time it took you to process the ad's message. No matter, you have made your decision. It is one of the actions listed below. But wait; first tell the standpoint from which you will defend your action. This is important because the set of assumptions under which you operate within a particular discourse community are bound to influence your decision. Then again, because you are simultaneously a member of multiple discourse communities, you may want to complicate your decision making by taking into account some of the multiple and conflicting assumptions that are operating in your case.

Action 1: Agree with Luke and Luke's analysis and shop for a different software program that positions you in a way your sensitivities can better tolerate.

Action 2: Admit that the grain of desire in the message has motivated you to buy the software, and walk to the checkout counter with your credit card in hand.

Action 3: Use whatever cultural resources (for example, humorous comeback to debunk the ad or negotiate its intended impact) that you have available for resisting Prodigy's *Amber*.

Action 4: Read the literature that discusses how different social groups are positioned by similar advertising campaigns, in terms of gender, race or ethnicity, and social class.

Reflection. Take a moment to name the set of assumptions that were operating when you chose one action over another. Were they consistent with those that were functioning when you responded to the two earlier scenarios? If not, what made this situation different?

Scenario Four

As a member of an advisory committee that assists the acquisitions librarian in your local public library make purchasing decisions, you find a list of periodicals for young adolescents under consideration. The list and an accompanying set of sample issues have been sent to you in advance of the committee's next meeting, which has been scheduled for 2 weeks from today. Your task is to read each sample issue from the list and evaluate its appropriateness for the adolescent population that the library serves. You notice that a note from the acquisitions librarian has been attached to the small stack of periodicals. It says the following:

> Please keep in mind that magazines for teens are generally read by much younger readers than the targeted audience. Although publishers do not typically acknowledge this fact, they do stand to gain from younger readers cutting their teeth on magazines that will continue to hold appeal in the years to come.

The following is the list of magazines for your consideration:

YM (Young and Modern)

Teen

Teen People

Seventeen

Jet

The Source

IN 2 PRINT

In looking over the sample issues of each of these magazines, you make the following notes:

1. *YM*, *Teen*, and *Seventeen* seem quite similar in what they offer. Articles on fashion, celebrity gossip, personal relationships, health and beauty aids, horoscopes, and entertainment are geared toward a female, mostly white, audience.

2. *Teen People* is billed as a new magazine for teens from the editors of *People*. It offers readers an opportunity to interact with their favorite stars online, and more. In the June/July 1998 issue of *Teen People*, readers are encouraged to look for the little red @ throughout the articles. It symbolizes some special happening on America Online (AOL) (key word "Teen People"). After logging on, *Teen People*

readers will find information on how they can contribute to future issues of the magazine, sign up for a weekly e-mail newsletter, win prizes, interact with their favorite stars in the magazine's weekly live auditoriums, and preview some new interactive video games.

3. *The Source*, which describes itself as the magazine of hip-hop music, culture, and politics, features articles aimed primarily at a male audience. For example, out of 14 letters to the editor, 12 were from males. One reader wrote the following:

> I have just one word to describe your article on the Goodie Mob: real. These brothers give the rap game just what it needs. They offer so much enlightenment with their righteous and spiritual form of rhyming. I am sure that the new album will do what the first one did, and that is wake up the knuckleheads that were sleeping. (Blak, 1998, p. 24)

4. The lead article in the June 1, 1998, issue of *Jet* is titled "Blacks Mourn Death of the Frank Sinatra That Nobody Knew." In this 10-page article (*Jet* is the size of *TV Guide*), Sinatra is described as "a man who stood up for the civil rights for Blacks and other minorities" (p. 6). There are short articles on sports, *Jet*'s top 20 albums and top 20 singles, television, health and beauty, politics, and lifestyles.

5. The Canadian magazine *IN 2 PRINT* has a different feel to it. The articles are the work of young people, and the magazine has a junior editorial staff. There are no advertisements for clothing, cosmetics, or personal hygiene products. Nor is the *t* word (teenager) used anywhere in the magazine, according to one respondent in her letter to the editor.

Decide which of the following actions you will take, and why. In which discourse community or communities are you claiming membership this time?

Action 1: Recommend that the entire list of magazines be purchased.

Action 2: Resign from the committee due to your inability to identify with any of the intended audiences.

Action 3: Do some action research on your own by asking adolescents whom you know to give their reactions to the magazines being considered.

Action 4: Go to the library and find some articles or books on adolescent audiences (their likes and dislikes, what they take pleasure in, how teen magazines position them).

Action 5: Suggest your own plan of action.

Reflection. Did you find yourself claiming membership in more than one discourse community? If so, how did that affect your choice of actions? Is it possible for you, personally, to speak from only one discourse community? Why or why not?

Moving On

If this chapter has succeeded in its invitation to think about the possibilities involved in teaching critical media literacy using popular culture, you are perhaps ready to explore further what such teaching might look like in your own classroom (or your imagined classroom, if you are not yet teaching). Or, perhaps you are still wondering what critical media literacy has to offer you as teacher, researcher, curriculum supervisor, or reading specialist. Alternatively, you may be taking a wait-and-see attitude—you do not have enough information yet to make a decision about the value of such a practice. Whatever the case, we think you will find Chapter 2 helpful in terms of its discussion of several approaches to teaching using popular culture and its in-depth look at the politics of pleasure in relation to both audience and teacher.

Approaches to Teaching Using Popular Culture and the Politics of Pleasure

Popular culture is difficult to pin down. Just when we memorize the words to a new song by the Spice Girls, become acquainted with the characters on television shows, or wear the latest spandex shirt and matching flair pants, the trends change. Our elementary knowledge of popular culture as adults and educators seems to lag behind the "real time" expertise and understanding of the youth and students we teach. So how are we as educators supposed to incorporate popular culture into critical media literacy practices when we are unsure that we are focusing on current and not outdated popular culture forms?

If we are able to momentarily capture an example of current popular culture to use in the classroom, the question then becomes what our role is in presenting this information. Are we as teachers supposed to be the interpreter of the information, calling attention to what we see from our adult perspectives to be the negative implications for our students? Or should we take on the role of bystander throwing out ideas and allowing students to determine the meanings on their own?

And if we are able to discern what our role as the teacher ought to be, then we must ask ourselves how we should broach this subject with students. Will they honestly and openly discuss with us in schools that which they hold sacred and important in their world outside the classroom? Or will they just pacify us as teachers and nod their heads in agreement, while keeping their real thoughts in the backs of their minds to later disclose to a friend during a phone conversation that night?

And should students decide to entrust their individual pleasures to others and engage in a discussion of popular culture in the classroom, especially with teachers who usually balk at or worry about students' preferences, are we as educators then obligated to validate each student's beliefs? How are we supposed to react to potentially differing views from the audience? And finally, if we are diligent enough to think through and successfully answer all of these questions, we are then confronted with yet one other dilemma: Once the tinder box of popular culture is opened in the educational setting, which examples of popular culture are actually admissible in the classroom? How do we determine which of the many forms and examples of popular culture are appropriate for exploration?

Teaching critical media literacy using popular culture may now seem like a daunting task with too many obstacles to overcome in order to include its study in classroom practice. However, with all good methodologies we must find weaknesses in the theory before we implement the practice. In this chapter we will discuss several complicated issues surrounding the selection, introduction, and discussion of popular culture framed by critical media literacy practices. Issues regarding the perspective of audience, the politics of pleasure, and the role of the teacher in relation to both pleasure and audience will be addressed.

Approaches to Teaching Using Popular Culture Texts

Before including popular culture texts of various forms in classroom instruction for students to dissect and critique, educators must realize the complex nature of their relevance and influence on students' lives. Through a discussion of four approaches to teaching critical media literacy, this chapter illustrates the various perspectives teachers have regarding popular culture's influence on students' lives.

In one approach educators all too often view popular culture as detrimental to youth and use critical media literacy activities as opportunities to expose students to the degradation of their young minds using examples of popular culture forms in which the students have shown interest. Carmen Luke (1997) believes that when teaching the critical study of popular culture as solely the uncovering of "false consciousness notions of ideology" (p. 41), then all media studies activities revert to notions of media as the root of evil and of students as mindless viewers. When teachers operate from this understanding, critical study of popular texts becomes an exercise in students' endurance of the teacher's proselytizing approach of warning students of the media's harmful effects. Any meanings that students produce from such texts are not factored into the learning scenario.

Take for example the "Turn Off the TV" week-long initiative that many schools have adopted to call attention to the amount of television students watch. What kind of message does this initiative send to students? On one hand, this activity allows children to assess the amount of time and the kinds of shows that they normally watch; however, it implicitly communicates to them that watching television—educational programs or otherwise—is not a productive way to spend time. Although this activity may force students to calculate the amount of television normally watched, it does not recognize the pleasures students encounter from these media texts, nor does it assist them in developing alternative opinions and perspectives from their normal television viewing. In essence, exposing students to such an activity, although well intended, may force students to go through the motions of the exercise while knowing that once the week is over they will turn on the television again.

Looking at media studies so narrowly limits the possibilities of what could be learned by both educators and students and distorts what is potentially a colorful picture into black and white. In this example, when educators choose to ignore the impact that popular culture forms have on students, they refuse to face the reality that all of us live in a postmodern society infiltrated with media and technology, and they neglect valuable opportunities to teach using these forms that inevitably and unavoidably surround us.

Teachers may implement a second approach to critical media literacy that involves recognizing the importance of popular culture in students' lives and including critical discourse practices in the classroom as a means of examining examples of popular texts.

This approach is likely to be used when teachers assume that students are thoughtlessly consuming popular culture. So in an effort to educate them, the teacher assumes the role of a liberating guide for students who passively take in all forms of popular culture that surround them. In this approach, students are taught how to critically analyze popular culture. They learn how to become "the ideal viewer...the one who is never persuaded or fooled, who sees through the illusions the media provide—in effect, the viewer who is impervious to influence" (Buckingham, 1993b, p. 146). In this approach, popular culture becomes an object of the curriculum for which a formulaic lesson taught by the teacher is used to scrutinize it. The media texts are critiqued devoid of any concern about the pleasures that students might derive from them. "Teaching about the media thus becomes a process of 'demystification,' of revealing underlying truths that are normally hidden from view" (Buckingham, 1998, p. 8). When this approach is implemented, popular culture forms are viewed as targets for analysis and any pleasures that students might associate with them are discounted and potentially destroyed.

To illustrate this strictly analytical approach to critical media literacy, it is helpful to reflect on an example.

> During a week of after-school bus duty, a sixth-grade English teacher notices several students thumbing through *Gamepro*, a video-game magazine, and overhears them conversing excitedly about their recent purchases of a newly released video game. The teacher gleans from the students' conversation that this game features eight female and male fighters who engage in mortal combat with one another. Every afternoon as the students wait for their bus to arrive, the teacher listens as they relentlessly discuss the moves they mastered the night before on their video-game machine and share with one another how to throw their opponent against the wall to win the fight.

> Concerned that the students are too consumed with the fighting in this virtual game, the teacher devises a lesson over the weekend to alert the students to the negative effects that the game has on their minds. On Monday during class, she explains that while at the grocery store over the weekend, she read in a new issue of *Gamepro* that the game was a hit with all ages. Then, for the next 40 minutes, she has the students engage in an activity to identify the violent elements of the game and to discuss their effects on students. By the end of the lesson, the students agree with the teacher that the game has skewed their understanding of

conflict and provided poor examples of problem solving. As the bell rings to change classes, the teacher smiles to herself, satisfied that the students have learned a valuable lesson about the detrimental effects of violent video games. However, the students leave the room thinking about how to maneuver the joystick to achieve a somersault kick that a fellow student had mentioned during the class discussion.

In this example, under the guise of critical media studies, "pedagogy becomes a tool leveled against students' pleasures derived from TV programs, from rock music, and popular culture more generally" (Luke, 1997, p. 41). As this example demonstrates, when a teacher takes this approach to media studies, students are quick to become protective of their actual thoughts and instead begin to read the text from what they perceive to be the teacher's perspective (Buckingham, 1993b). Such an approach thwarts the potential for genuine critical thinking.

A third approach to critical media literacy emphasizes the pleasures that popular culture can provide students. When exploring critical literacy practices in this way, teachers pay close attention to students' perceptions and liking of the popular culture forms brought into the classroom, and they are careful not to force students to analyze and critique that which they like. However, this approach also has its drawbacks. Students who are not encouraged to look at popular media from a more discerning perspective are left without having their perspectives challenged or explored more deeply (Britzman, 1991). Furthermore, when concern for students' pleasures override all other interests, critical media literacy education falls prey to validating individual students' pleasures and differences without building on and improving their critique of the media (Buckingham, 1993b). A turn to focusing on a totality of differences in pleasures runs the risk of undermining any common ground from which to build a curriculum of moral, social, and ethical standing. When this occurs, "views and voices from everywhere are potentially views and voices from nowhere" (Luke, 1998, p. 25).

To illustrate this point of pleasures without parameters, a situation devoid of thoughtful reflection on the media's impact on students' identities, think about how the teacher in the following example uses students' pleasures in his lesson.

As the culminating activity of a literature unit on fairy tales, a third-grade teacher has his students write their own fairy-tale stories. During writer's workshop for the next several weeks, the students draft and illustrate their own fairy tales complete with detailed characters and descriptive story lines. The teacher observes that the children draw from their understanding of both classic and contemporary fairy tales shared during the unit as well as from other formats such as Walt Disney movies. During writing conferences with the students, the teacher listens to story summaries of their work in progress and notes their enthusiasm with the project. Wanting to respect the students' ideas, perspectives, and expertise, he provides assistance only in sentence structure and spelling.

Upon completion, the children share their stories with the class audience. As the stories are read aloud by the students, the teacher realizes that almost all the children wrote traditional stories with male heroes who save long-haired damsels in distress so that they can live happily ever after. The teacher thinks to himself that although the students had read contemporary, nontraditional tales during the unit, only two children emulated those story lines in their own writing. Attributing this to student differences and personal interests, the teacher decides not to discuss this matter with the students and instead congratulates them on their hard work. Then all the books are published and put into the classroom library.

In this example, the students' pleasures drive the teacher's decisions not to discuss alternative readings of the popular fairy tales. And, although the teacher has incorporated nontraditional texts into the fairy-tale unit, he does not explicitly discuss the differences between the traditional and contemporary story images. Hence, the teacher in this scenario becomes "little more than a 'senior colleague' who engages students in an 'equal dialogue,' rather than an authority whose perspective is necessarily privileged" (Masterman as cited in Buckingham, 1998, p. 4). The students' pleasures are celebrated without any opportunity for further exploration or understanding of multiple pleasures from the contemporary texts. When teaching practices such as these are implemented, teachers do nothing more than leave students where they are (Buckingham, 1993b).

A fourth approach to popular culture studies has been developed from a combination of the approaches mentioned previously. Grounded in feminism, postmodernism, and cultural studies, this approach attempts to address the issues of analysis, pleasure, positioning, and audience so that a balance is created in the classroom. Using an aggregate approach, teachers recognize popular culture as a real, authentic, and influencing part of students' lives, holistic and separate from their school experiences and from the adults around them (Buckingham, 1998; Luke, 1997). Therefore, teachers acknowledge several crucial points: the expertise that students bring to the learning environment, the pleasures that popular culture produce for students, and the multiple readings that students produce from popular culture. But within this approach, teachers also embed the critical analysis of media texts to enable students to read from broader perspectives.

Weaving together these approaches, several researchers argue for a pedagogy of media studies that is self-reflexive (Buckingham, 1998; Ellsworth, 1989; C. Luke, 1994). Drawing from commonalities in feminism and cultural studies, this approach stresses individual differences and multiple reading positions as well as situation-specific critical deconstruction of media texts. Furthermore, postmodernism calls attention to the locality of the audience and to individual differences within the audience. All this leads to an approach to teaching in which there is "a constant movement back and forth between practice and theory, between celebration and critical analysis, and between language use and language study" (Buckingham, 1993b, p. 151).

This self-reflexive approach also builds on a commitment to the global realm of critical studies (Luke & Roe, 1993). From this perspective, it is not enough for teachers to stress the microanalysis of popular culture within the classroom structure. Rather, teachers need to provide opportunities for students to explore the issues of "how media and the mass-produced icons of popular culture situate us into relations of power by shaping our emotional, political, social, and material lives" (Luke & Roe, 1993, p. 118). Therefore, a balance must emerge so that critical media literacy is not purely a cognitive experience, nor is it solely experiencing pleasures without challenges to extend learning.

In order to practice self-reflexive teaching and learning and to provide students opportunities both to discuss the pleasures derived from popular culture and to read the texts from various and perhaps oppositional positions, we need to examine the concept of audience and the politics of pleasure before bringing the two together in the classroom. A closer look at each of these elements and the teacher's role in relation to audience and pleasures will assist in further developing our adult conceptions of popular culture and its place in classrooms where critical media literacy is practiced.

Audience and Popular Culture

From a behaviorist and traditional standpoint, audiences were thought to be passive spectators taking in various media forms without filtering, judging, or necessarily choosing them. It was assumed that children received all the images, especially televisual images, without any forethought; moreover, such images (mostly negative) were believed to adversely affect children's understanding of the world. From this perspective, the media was viewed as transmitting meanings to the audience by forcing onto them the ideologies it espoused. It was said that the media preceded the audience. In other words, the audience received information from the media and could not see through the propaganda.

However, this transmission model has been replaced with constructivist views that audiences are not made up of mindless consumers they were once thought to be. Several issues become visible within this revised framework. First, the audience brings prior knowledge and experiences to an interaction with media texts. Second, in conjunction with preexisting knowledge, the audience actively constructs meaning and derives pleasures from media texts; and because of each individual's prior knowledge, multiple meanings or pleasures of the text may be read. Third, through this active construction of meaning, the audience is capable of making judgments and evaluating ideology presented by the media. And finally, the audience is socially situated and context specific (Fiske, 1994). That is, the construction of meaning and pleasures depends on the knowledge of a particular group at a particular time and about a particular popular culture text. Audience interactions with popular culture are not static but always changing depending on the audience members and the situation.

Although the notion of audience has shifted from passive to active, the concept of students' expertise in dealing with popular culture texts remains problematic. For some, such as Fiske (1989b), discussion of the audience's expertise is irrelevant. According to Fiske's theory, the audience, as the subordinate, will always attempt to subvert the meanings associated with the dominant view. However, there are others (for example, Buckingham, 1998; Dyson, 1997; Luke, 1997) who disagree with this notion. While recognizing that audiences *do* construct meaning as a group but also construct their *own* meaning based on their individual background knowledge, these theorists and researchers believe that audiences need to be taught how to look at media images through lenses other than those presented by the media's ideological portrayals. The concern here centers around the belief that although audiences are actively constructing meaning from and indulging in pleasures of popular culture, there is no assurance that they are making meaning that goes beyond their own expert understanding.

For example, Moss (1993) studied this problem of student expertise in relation to audiences actively making meaning of the media. From her research on 7- to 12-year-old boys and girls talking about horror movies, she concluded that children learned how to construct meaning from media texts not only by paying attention to the text as experts but, more importantly, by talking about it with others. Through discussions of horror movies, Moss found that children constructed meaning of the texts through social practices during and after the text interaction. Her findings also revealed that children used discussions of texts to understand their position in the audience (in this case as adult or child), to construct their knowledge of the text genre, and to negotiate what constituted horror in the group's minds. Moss concluded that a reader-centered approach to audiences whereby "readers learn how to read from other readers, as well as the text" (p. 179) best captures the social interaction crucial to students' active construction of meaning. Similarly, Lewis (1998) advocated for audience discussion of popular culture texts in the classroom because, as she stated, "The popular culture of young people is not about individual voices and identities. At the local level, in classrooms and communities, popular culture is related to social and cultural group identities, allegiances, and exclusions" (p. 118).

As we have seen, audiences are active groups who approach popular culture with a pre-formed conception of who they are and what they believe as a group and as individuals. Using information that they share socially, they explore their own pleasures and construct new meanings from texts. However, as educators we also should realize that "to acknowledge the complexity and diversity of children's existing knowledge of the media is not to suggest that they have nothing to learn, nor that we have nothing to teach them" (Buckingham, 1993b, p. 150). It is by recognizing the existing pleasures of the audience and by soliciting the audience's knowledge that we can delve into those pleasures and assist students in developing their understanding and appreciation of multiple readings of popular culture texts. We now turn to the pleasures of popular culture texts to explore their significance in relation to students' enjoyment.

The Politics of Pleasure

According to Fiske (1989b), popular culture is conflicting by nature because it celebrates the meanings and beliefs of subordinated groups while opposing the beliefs of the dominant. Because popular culture centers around the interests of students (the subordinated) and is perhaps in opposition to the beliefs of teachers (the dominant), teachers must carefully approach the conflictual nature of media studies when considering its use in the classroom. When popular culture is included in classroom practice, it is at risk of "being purified, homogenized, and reconstituted as curriculum or motivational strategies" (Grace & Tobin, 1998, p. 46). Working from a self-reflexive framework, teachers must be aware of the tenuous relation between students' pleasures from, and analysis of, popular culture. They also must be cognizant of the struggle that often emerges as a result of committing to both the pleasure principle and the process of critical analysis. Establishing an understanding of the importance of pleasure builds awareness of its relevance to students' lives and assists teachers in developing curricula that not only recognize but also challenge students to think beyond the pleasures derived from popular culture texts.

Pleasures constitute a major component of popular culture and are expressive of the likes of students. According to Barthes (1975), pleasures of texts may be represented through experiences of *jouissance* and *plaisir*. To Barthes, *jouissance* is a heightened state of extreme pleasure reserved for special moments when participants lose themselves fully in the consumption of a text. The intensity of interaction between the text and participant intermingles these two components such that meaning for the participant is defined only within that particular moment in time, which renders the encounter as unspeakable to others. It is "not about confirming or reproducing dominant power-relationships and values; on the contrary, it involves a form of liberation from such constraints" (Buckingham, 1998, p. 66). To illustrate the concept of jouissance, Fiske (1989b) described adolescents losing themselves in rock music played so loudly that the experience becomes one of total body involvement. In this instance, the act of *listening* to music changes to an act of *experiencing* the music. *Plaisir*, according to Barthes, encompasses a different kind of pleasure. It is the enjoyment of a social experience occurring more often and less intensely than jouissance, and one in which participants are able to separate themselves from their pleasures and to discuss their feelings with others. It is "seen as a situation in which rules can be broken and more powerful identities assumed, if only on the level of fantasy" (Buckingham, 1998, p. 66). To further illustrate Fiske's example, one might say that plaisir would involve listening to a song at a lower volume level and then being able to tell others the pleasures had from it.

Drawing from Barthes's ideas, Fiske (1989b) asserted that in relation to popular culture, jouissance becomes the pleasure of evading and resisting ideology and can neither be analyzed nor separated from the experience because it is context specific; conversely, plaisir is associated with socially produced group pleasures related to the dominant ideology. Grace and Tobin (1998) took Fiske's idea one step further in their research with third-grade students involved in a video production activity. They associated students' plaisir of media studies with "having fun" within sanctioned school parameters developed and overseen by adults. And they likened jouissance to moments of students' video production and viewing when they "were united in a spirit of camaraderie, a celebration of otherness organized around laughter" (p. 54), and when the teachers in attendance were momentarily shut out of the reveling intensity had by the children. Recognizing the difference between the two kinds of pleasures, the teachers concluded from their work with these students that critical media studies projects initiated in classrooms need to allow time for both jouissance and plaisir, and that overall the teacher's goal "should be to validate the popular culture interests of children without appropriating them" (Grace & Tobin, 1998, pp. 46–47).

Buckingham's (1993c) work with 12- to 15-year-old students' pleasures of computer games also illustrates this difference between plaisir and jouissance. Although girls in this study owned video games and enjoyed playing them, they were able only to reflect, verbalize, and critique the pleasures they associated with the game playing, thus engaging in plaisir. The boys, on the other hand, had a more difficult time communicating their pleasurable experiences of video games. Buckingham noted that "they were almost too close to the experience, and for this reason they could only define it in insiders' terms" (p. 24), thus exemplifying the jouissance of the video-playing pleasures of these adolescent boys.

Although pleasures and play with popular culture texts connote enjoyment, they also may be problematic. Just as we need to recognize the power of pleasure to evoke feelings of jouissance and plaisir, we also need to understand that these pleasures are not always universal within a group. In other words, multiple and perhaps oppositional readings of the same popular culture texts result from the readings of the individual. This poses both positive and negative implications for educators. Knowing that popular culture evokes multiple interpretations will undoubtedly improve discussions as students will more likely want to voice their own perspectives and opinions; however, any one perspective shared with the group has the potential to be opposed by any other perspective within the group. The pleasures elicited from readings of popular culture may vary among students, and what one student may find pleasurable may be offensive to someone else. This includes pleasures perceived to be offensive among students or those enjoyed by students but found to be offensive to teachers.

For example, during a conversation Margaret had with a group of eighth-grade girls and boys about their favorite recent movies, the group began discussing the movie *Billy Madison*. Laughing hysterically, the children retold the story to Margaret.

Frances: It's this movie about a dumb guy who does really dumb things for a grown man to do...like he acts like a kid and he is a total idiot but it is hilarious. He does things like talks to inanimate objects.

Sabrina:	Yeah, it is so funny because he is really stupid and he never finished school. You know he is just one of those really dumb guys.
Frances:	But then he decides to go back [to school]. And it is so funny because he has to go back through every grade because he is so dumb. Like he starts in first grade and goes through twelfth grade.
Quentin:	Then he graduates from high school and decides to go to college and become a teacher. It is just funny because, you know, like you're glad he is going to be a teacher but you really cannot imagine what kind of teacher he is going to be.
Rod:	Yeah—some teachers are just like that though (laughter). Like, hey Billy Madison really *is* my science teacher…just a really stupid guy.

(Laughter and agreement among the students).

Interestingly, these students knew that Margaret was a teacher, but they did not have a problem sharing with her their pleasures of the movie because this character was an imbecile and decided to become a teacher. Based on their retelling, Margaret thought to herself that she would not find the same pleasures in the movie because its portrayal of an idiot as an educator offended her.

Pleasures from popular culture texts also may be offensive between and among students. Just because a text may be considered popular does not ensure that it will be enjoyed by everyone in the group. For example, consider the following scenario.

Four-seventh grade boys are collaborating on a writing activity in which they are to compose a newspaper article for their class newspaper. Their teacher had told them that the article could be fictitious but needed to include the five Ws (who, what, when, where, why). These boys discussed several possible topics that were of interest to them, including clothing, sports, video games, music, and movies. In the end, they decided to write an article about the band Mötley Crüe. In their short draft, they described the music of this hard-rock band and detailed each of the band members, highlighting in particular Tommy Lee (the drummer), who is known for his ability to twirl his drumsticks while playing. When the students finished their draft, they took it to their proofreading buddies, a different group of boys, who read it over for them. Two of the proofreaders verbalized their disapproval of the article for the class newspaper because they considered Tommy Lee to be a woman hater (he had been sentenced to jail for beating his wife). Consequently, they recommended that the Mötley Crüe fans should not publish their article in the paper because the band was offensive. The boys who had written the article stated that they already knew this about Tommy Lee, but they still thought that Mötley Crüe was the greatest band and that Tommy was cool. They decided to submit the article to the paper against the protest of their proofreading counterparts.

As illustrated by these two examples, pleasures of popular culture are not always universal and can present problems within a group. At the same time, differences in pleasures are not always negative and actually can be used in classroom settings to explore students' multiple readings of popular culture texts.

Extending Understanding Through Pleasures

As mentioned earlier, critical media literacy is much more than a celebration of pleasures. Although identification and enjoyment of pleasures is an important aspect of teaching critical media literacy, it is only part of the picture. Certainly, its place in the curriculum is important in order to validate students' understanding and the meanings they have attached to popular culture texts. But pleasures derived from popular culture are also noteworthy because they are complicated and at times uncomfortable, and it is through the exploration of these various pleasures that students may take a more in-depth look at popular culture and ponder other possibilities and positions of political, social, and cultural relevance that they have not examined before.

The purpose of critical media literacy then should be not to destroy pleasures but to explore them to uncover new and different forms of enjoyment (Masterman, 1985). A movement to critical practices should open possibilities for other readings and productions of popular texts without dismissing the pleasures already formed. And when these opportunities are explored, teachers must acknowledge that students may develop positions that are different from the ones that we would like them to form. Through parody and imitation of popular culture texts, Lewis (1998) and Buckingham (1998) found that students use their pleasures to examine their own understandings of the world and to develop new ones.

To illustrate this, we turn to Lewis's (1998) examination of a group of ten 11- to 12-year-old boys whose book talk illustrates how they use parody to examine their pleasures of horror texts (in this case the book *Bobby's Back*) as well as to explore their feelings of fear associated with this popular genre (making connections with other horror characters from movies). An excerpt of their discussion follows:

Brian:	Jason's better than Freddy. Jason kills more people. One movie he kills like 15 people. The most Freddy ever killed was five, six.
James:	They run from him and they get like a mile away, and then they turn around and he's right there and he's just walking.
Tyler:	Who cares who kills more people?
Brian:	Jason does not even act real.
	[some text omitted]
James:	Jason's better. He carries a chain saw.
Student:	It's really scary.
Mark:	Not always. He uses anything he can find.
Brian:	Free Willy scared me.
Tyler:	Free Willy versus Jaws.
Sam:	Care Bears scared me.
	[some text omitted]
Brian:	The Smurfs versus Jason.... The Flintstones could bash his face in.
James:	Bam Bam Bam Bam.
Sam:	Willy versus Shamu.
James:	Tyler versus Mark.
Brian:	Free Willy versus Jaws.
Brian:	Mark versus Tyler.

As Lewis (1998, p. 117) noted as an observer, she initially did not think that the students' conversation was productive; however, after further observation she asserted that it is through the parody of this exchange that perhaps these boys were able to explore their own fears in a culture where being male is associated with fearlessness. In essence, the students were able to use their pleasures of popular culture to make meaning for themselves. As a teacher, allowing students this sort of conversational transgression in the classroom may feel uncomfortable; as Lewis pointed out, regular discussions such as these without a teacher's guidance do not assist children in exploring other issues of critical media literacy. But in conclusion, Lewis advocated for classroom practices that provide times for student discussions of popular culture, both with and without teacher input.

Other common concerns with the pleasures of popular culture involve the imitation of the popular in students' construction of media texts. It could be argued that the students in Lewis's study were only imitating the negative effects of the influence of the horror genre on their understanding when they positioned one child against the other (for example, "Mark versus Tyler"). But Lewis addressed this issue, as well, explaining that the boys were engaging in a subversive activity that opposed the norms held by the classroom structure. Their use of the language may look like imitation of the ideology of horror to an observer, but it may be used, as in this example, to explore group identities.

Buckingham (1998) agreed that imitation of popular culture does not necessarily mean that students are mindlessly reproducing the ideology that we as teachers are trying to get them to understand better from other positions. It is through this kind of safe imitation, or what looks to be imitation, that students may actually be trying on new positions and identities that they had only imagined previously. Parody, then, "can function as a critical mode in its own right, which provides access to the parts that more closed forms of analysis cannot reach" (Buckingham, 1998, p. 70). Furthermore, critical media literacy should entail what Morgan (1998) called the "making and remaking [of media texts] rather than merely as texts for decipherment" (p. 128). In other words, imitation needs to be viewed as both involvement in pleasures as well as the deconstruction of its meaning to assist students in "teasing out" the pleasures and reflecting on what they learned from the experience (Buckingham, 1998; Buckingham & Sefton-Green, 1994).

The Teacher's Role: Putting It All Together

So how do we negotiate the tension between pleasure and critical awareness so that critical media literacy can be successfully discussed, explored, played with, and taught in classrooms? Luke (1998) believed that teachers need to seriously consider the different readings and pleasures that students associate with popular culture, but she cautioned teachers against an overreliance on students' personal response. Suggesting that a balance must emerge between pleasures and analysis of texts, she stated, "the point is that a critical cultural and social literacy, one that includes a critical understanding of media texts, industries, and the production of meaning, must balance discourse critique with giving students opportunities for alternative readings and text productions" (p. 41).

To balance the components of active audiencing, individual pleasures, and critical literacy, we suggest that teachers consider several issues. These include a practice based on materials relevant to students' lives, a commitment to students' pleasures and to critical awareness, and flexible teaching practices that allow for teachers to take on multiple roles within the context of a single lesson.

Curriculum Built on Relevance

In order for texts to be used for critical media literacy practices, they must be relevant to the audience. Relevancy "requires connections between the texts and the social experience of the reader that precedes it" (Fiske, 1989a, p. 186). Audiences must be interested in reading the texts and finding pleasures in them in order for relevancy to exist, and what is relevant to one group may be irrelevant to another. Therefore, it is essential that when choosing popular culture texts to use in the classroom, the choices are based on the students' own experiences and identities so that learning does not just become another curricular experience (Buckingham, 1993b; C. Luke, 1994). If teachers choose texts without knowledge of the students' interests or pleasures, students may not find relevance in them. And "if there are no relevances between a text and the everyday lives of its readers, there will be little motivation to read it and less pleasure to be gained from doing so" (Fiske, 1989a, p. 187). Furthermore it is only through pleasures of relevant popular culture in students' lives that we will be able to begin further inquiry into their political and social interests and make connections to larger social, economic, and political meanings (C. Luke, 1994).

Commitment to Pleasure and Critical Media Literacy

As we discussed earlier in this chapter, the celebration of students' pleasures and differences in active construction of meaning by audiences and in individual pleasures of its members is essential to understanding the importance of popular culture in students' lives. And, although these differences in pleasures may improve a lesson's discussion and uncover new meaning, pleasures also may be problematic because of those differences (Britzman, 1991; Ellsworth, 1989). To address these difficulties, Luke (1997) cautioned that just because students have different and unique readings of popular culture does not necessarily mean that "anything goes" (p. 47). Luke argued that because multiple and different readings are desirable but also problematic, educators must provide opportunities for students to encounter their own realizations about social justice and equity of people. Instead of forcing students to practice what we believe to be true or correct, a better approach would be for educators to guide students through a process of learning how to question their own pleasures.

Similarly, Dyson (1997) recommended that teachers adopt a "pedagogy of responsibility" (p. 180) to address differences. In a year-long study of second graders' use of popular culture in their writing, she concluded that students need to have opportunities to create, share, and discuss their ideas in a classroom environment shaped by "an ethic of inclusion and a sensitivity to collective exclusion" (p. 180).

Because it is the educator's responsibility to monitor the inclusion of popular culture practices in the classroom, we look finally at the multiple roles teachers must assume to address relevancy of pleasures, critical awareness of texts, and a commitment of responsible actions from a self-reflexive position.

Flexible Roles

Teaching about popular culture using critical media literacy is more than a process of *just* teaching or *just* learning. It is a complex set of issues through which "we need to find a pathway between a host of polarities pervasive within media pedagogy: critical versus duped, autonomous versus controlled, rational versus emotional, active versus passive" (Morgan, 1998, p. 122). To find our way through this entanglement of opposites, Green (1998) suggested that teachers view their role as one of negotiation. Combining negotiation with a self-reflexive approach to teaching, educators might assume several roles in order to address the issues that surround the audience, pleasure, and critique of popular culture that have been discussed in this chapter. These roles, although presented in a linear manner, are not linear at all. Teachers move in and out of them fluidly depending on the needs of the students in the classroom.

One role that teachers might assume is that of learner, especially when they call on students to share their interests and pleasures in popular culture texts. While learning, teachers are the neophytes and their students become the experts. A guide is a second role that teachers might assume. As a guide, teachers assist students in identifying and critiquing popular culture texts. In this way, teachers are not the transmitters of information to a passive audience; instead by readily placing themselves alongside their students, both students and teachers become agents of change (Richards, 1998). And finally, teachers must at some point assume the role of authority, because as Carmen Luke (1994) has argued, it is at times unavoidable and politically necessary in order to ensure that students' pleasures are respected and questioned.

Concluding Remarks

This chapter began with questions about the implementation of critical media literacy using popular culture in the classroom. We hope that the discussion of the approaches to teaching using popular culture and of the issues that surround the politics of pleasure and audience has been helpful in answering some of these questions. As you read the lessons that are presented in Chapters 3, 4, and 5, we encourage you to reflect on this information and consider how pleasures, audience, and the role of the teacher influenced each lesson's structure and the outcomes.

CHAPTER 3

Engaging Primary Grade Students in Critical Media Literacy: Jennifer's Lesson

As a former primary classroom teacher in New York City, I can recall many times during writing workshop when the students seemed to be more interested in the latest *Power Rangers* episode they had seen on television than they were in the more traditional and "school-appropriate" topics we had discussed earlier during the minilesson phase of writing workshop. Although children were free to talk and write about any topic of their choice, I became uneasy when page after page of their journals filled with Power Rangers and other superheroes. I was looking for topics that were safely within the boundaries of school and family, such as children's memories of happy and unhappy incidents growing up, friendships in and out of school, or ideas learned from field trips around the city. At the time, I was reluctant to accept the children's popular culture fantasies as a legitimate topic to be valued and studied in my classroom. Like many educators, I was an advocate for the "turn off the television and turn on to books" pedagogy, and believed that television, video games, and the media at large were foes that teachers had to fight in our efforts to stop the declining scores on tests of children's literacy skills. Back then, I considered myself to be a progressive new teacher who had a child-centered, student empowering teaching philosophy. I tried to encourage free choice by my students whenever possible.

However, simply allowing students to write about superheroes during "free" writing time and not consciously addressing how they are understanding these popular culture texts are minimal in the range of activities that teachers can take on when they decide to use popular culture texts to teach critical media literacy. In other words, free exploration can be a beginning to a critical media literacy lesson, but it should not stop there. It is important that teachers take time to consider their positions on using popular culture in the classroom and negotiate how critical media literacy might be used to teach primary school children about understanding their world.

How the Lesson Was Constructed

In May 1998, I sat with two groups of second-grade students for about 40 minutes each to do a lesson I had developed. The lesson was called "Drawing Me as the Perfect Superhero." It was a modified version of a lesson that Cohen (1998) had done with primary students in Australia. The focus of the lesson was to examine how young children can be helped to "explore more directly the imaginings which could be mobilized in constructing a multi- rather than mono-cultural image/text" (p. 168).

In Cohen's example, a small group of students worked together to create what became the "Indian Cowgirl Warrior," a figure embodying various features that represented the children's diverse cultural backgrounds. Although I used Cohen's idea for my lesson, I did make several changes in adapting it for use with popular culture texts. The purpose of my lesson was to provide primary grade students with an opportunity to explore their knowledge about superheroes and to construct their self-identity through their perceptions of what it would be like to be the perfect superhero. I designed the lesson so that each student could work individually to draw from his or her resources on the topic of superheroes. I was especially interested in what they valued and found to be desirable characteristics of these superheroes. I also was interested in how the children would interact with one another during their creation of the perfect superhero picture text.

Thinking Through the Lesson and Positioning Myself in It

Before doing the lesson, I was a bit nervous and worried that it might not be successful. Aside from having a flexible plan of what I would like the students to do, I was not certain how the lesson was going to turn out. Also, I knew that my other purpose for doing the lesson involved observing, thinking, and analyzing the identity/image construction process *during* the lesson. This meant that I would have to concentrate on teaching and observing simultaneously. In the end, I wanted to be able to offer suggestions for how teachers might use a critical media literacy lesson in a primary classroom. Because I knew that I needed to keep myself open to any unexpected turn in the lesson, I decided to position myself as someone between a friend and a teacher. This would help the children see me as someone they could feel comfortable enough to speak to honestly, but also as someone who would still maintain responsibility for taking control if necessary. To me, this seemed the best way to maintain a balance between openness/freedom and structure/control.

As I sat with the students around a small table, the uncertainties and doubts about the purposeful "looseness" of my lesson plan worried me considerably. I was new to this group. How would they receive me and my ideas? As soon as I told the first group of students that we were going to do an activity on superheroes, their eyes lit up and a smile came across the faces of these students who a moment earlier were sitting with dull and uneasy expressions. I knew the lesson would work well.

Two Small-Group Lessons

Lesson One

In the first small group, there were four students—one girl and three boys. Two were African Americans, one was of European American background, and one was from Brazil. I first asked these four students to name any superheroes they knew and liked. As they called out names enthusiastically, I wrote the following list:

Superman
Little Robin
Batman
Peter Pan
Hercules ("the Walt Disney one")
Mortal Kombat Jack
Sub-Zero
Superfriends
X-Men, Wolverine, Storm, Professor X
Silver Surfer
Fantastic Four

I was somewhat surprised by how unchanged and long lasting some of the favorite superhero characters seemed to be. As I wrote in Chapter 1, I grew up watching the Fantastic Four, X-Men, and most of the other superheroes the children named. Because I was a bit surprised to find the children talking about these "old" and possibly "outdated" superheroes, I decided to try and tap into their current knowledge. I asked them who their favorite characters were from the television comedy show *South Park*. With the exception of the one girl in the group, no one else had heard of *South Park*. The girl who knew about it said that most children were "too young to stay up that late" to watch it. She stated that her father videotaped every episode.

For the most part, the students' knowledge of popular culture was defined by cable television, the Cartoon Network, the Nickelodeon channel, and the comic books they or their older siblings read. *South Park* was outside their immediate access and therefore was not a part of their world, contrary to what one might think from reading current magazines about the show's popularity among children. This caused me to reflect on the assumptions that adults may have about children's knowledge of popular culture. Teachers who use popular culture texts in their classrooms may not assume anything about their students' knowledge and taste. The practical implication to be gleaned from this is that any informed decision about selecting curriculum materials or popular culture texts for literacy lessons must be made in collaboration with the students. Their comments made me realize the importance of having access to certain information. This also made me question any assumption I might have had about grouping them as young consumers who automatically knew about the latest popular culture phenomenon.

I was particularly struck by the quiet and orderly atmosphere of the classroom lesson. I was ready for anything to happen, even the possibility of a few imaginative kids jumping off the table to "fly." The students were mostly engrossed in their own creations, and looked up only once in awhile to answer one another's questions or to look at one another's work. There were fewer verbal interactions among the students in the group than I expected. This may have been due to various reasons, but most particularly to the instructions I gave that they should draw their own images individually.

I did not observe any obvious power struggles among the students. For example, I did not notice anyone in the group who tried to establish dominance for a certain superhero. Nor did I notice any difference among the students' competence to work successfully and complete the task at hand. In fact, none of the students had any trouble or doubts about being able to create a picture text of their perfect superhero.

When I began the lesson, I had worried about my decision not to bring in any visuals to give students ideas. I had decided that it might be better not to provide any visuals because I did not know the students' taste in popular culture texts, and I even feared that I might influence their choices by showing images of some superheroes and not others. As it turned out, I had no reason to be concerned; the students had no trouble choosing and drawing their superheroes. In fact, their perfect superheroes were all quite unique.

Before they began their picture texts, I asked them to imagine themselves as the perfect superheroes. We discussed what would make a superhero perfect to them. Some of their responses were "He has to be strong and able to carry heavy things," and "He has to fly or do something that we can't do." Then, I showed them an outline of a figure and pointed out how they might take different aspects that they admired in different superheroes to construct a perfect superhero. For example, they could draw the head, arms, body, and legs from different superheroes, depending on the particular features or powers they wished they could have. The students responded by simply saying "cool," and began to draw. As they drew, I asked them to talk about why they chose certain superheroes to construct their own

Table 1
Conversation During the "Drawing Me as the Perfect Superhero" Activity

Jen (author)	Pilar (age 7)	Dougdrick (age 8)	Martin (age 7)	Chris (age 8)
"What are you drawing?"	"The head is like this cartoon person Zorax."	"I'm drawing Superman because he's superhero—the strongness!" (flexes his arm to show a muscle.)		"I'm a cross between Eagleman—he's got wings and invincible, and Superman's body because he's like really, really strong."
"What are you drawing now?"			"I have a Aquaman's head and he can hold breath for so long." "The arms are Hercules because he's strong. The feet are Wolverine's because he's cool."	"I have Wolverine's legs too because they're strong legs."

(continued)

Table 1
Conversation During the "Drawing Me as the Perfect Superhero" Activity (continued)

Jen (author)	Pilar (age 7)	Dougdrick (age 8)	Martin (age 7)	Chris (age 8)
"Is it important for superheroes to be strong?"				"I like them to be strong because I'm strong—I can pick up three people at a time."
	"I'm making mine as Pegasus, Hercules, and Zorax because they're funny."		"I'm Aquaman and he can talk with sea creatures. It's kind of weird."	My face is like the Darkman. It's a cool mask."
		(To Chris) "You talking about the mask of Zorro?		No—it's Darkman, a cartoon."

(continued)

Table 1

Conversation During the "Drawing Me as the Perfect Superhero" Activity (continued)

Jen (author)	Pilar (age 7)	Dougdrick (age 8)	Martin (age 7)	Chris (age 8)
"Explain weird."		"From Mortal Kombat. He's weird, part animal, part human."	"I remember Ninja Turtles."	"That's a hard question. Hmm. He's not invincible but not capable of dying. Like Superman —he never dies. Eagleman, he doesn't even have a way of dying. Even if you shoot with a cannon."
"Are you afraid of dying?"	"I'm not."			"I'm afraid of everything dying— my pet Rascal dying. Who isn't afraid of dying? I'm not afraid of heart attack, but BB guns, bombs, or old age—I don't know...."

perfect superhero. I recorded their responses and the conversations among the group members as they were drawing themselves. Table 1 on pages 46–48 shows a partial sample of their discussions.

As Table 1 indicates, I asked questions while the students worked. I tried to make my questions specific to each child's work, and especially to follow up on their earlier comments. It was clear from analyzing their responses that the students considered me to be the audience, and they performed accordingly. They answered my questions and they worked as they were asked to do. This is important because it demonstrates the positioning that was going on during this lesson. Although I wanted to present myself as the quasi-teacher-friend, I may have been positioned by the students as just another teacher who wanted them to perform a particular task. On the other hand, they may have positioned me as a "cool" adult who knew quite a bit about their world. Depending on these two possibilities or on the many other ways that they may have positioned me, they could have done one of the following: rejected the lesson, performed the lesson in the way they viewed as being appropriate for the school context, or simply explored their understanding of their world of superheroes as they knew it. It appeared to me that they enjoyed the lesson as a genuine exploration, although there is no clear evidence that what they performed for me was how they would have chosen to portray themselves if I had not been present or if the context had been their homes.

READING INTO SUPERHEROES.　In doing the activity, some of the students constructed themselves as superheroes more readily than others. For instance, Martin was only satisfied with his fourth attempt, and others drew, erased, and then drew again, as they negotiated their image. As shown in Table 1, the discussion leaned heavily in the direction of death as a theme, at least for one of the students. This was something that I had not expected.

CHRIS: STRENGTH, DEATH, AND IMMORTALITY.　Through conversations while engaged in the activity, Chris revealed a concern that seemed serious and sensitive, but one that I suppose every student thinks about from time to time. He connected his fear of death with the death of a relative that affected him when he was younger. He stated that he probably was afraid of dying and losing his loved ones (like his pet rat Rascal) because he once had experienced someone close to him

Figure 2
Chris's Superhero

dying. Although I did not get a chance to interview Chris individually after the lesson, I can see how his fear of death had manifested itself in his construction of himself as the perfect superhero. By picturing himself as someone who could not die (such as Superman or Eagle-man), he was borrowing powers that enabled him to compensate for a situation in which he felt powerless and vulnerable (see Figure 2).

During this lesson and while observing other students construct their perfect superheroes, I realized the lure and the power of allowing students to express themselves through the use of popular culture texts. The students were deeply involved in the construction of their fantasy superheroes. More often than not, they were the experts who gave one another information and feedback, while I, the teacher, was very much an observer. They were very much in charge, and they conducted a work session that I could not have led better myself.

Lesson Two

Aside from strength and immortality being important necessities of superheroes, other desirable features came out in the work of the second small group of children. This group was composed of one girl and three boys. Two of the children were of European American heritage, one was African American, and the other was Chinese. Just as in the first group, the students in this second group were unique in their interpretation and adaptation of the activity. For instance, Beau constructed himself as three different heroes, rather than one (see Figure 3 on page 52).

BEAU: PERSONALIZING AND "OWNING" THE ACTIVITY. Beau drew Flash, Spiderman, and Superman separately to indicate that he can transform himself into three different superheroes, as desired. Not being satisfied with my instructions to combine several superheroes and embody them as one, Beau drew his own interpretation of the assignment. As with any literary responses or creation of text, some students will interpret the assignment in very different ways to fit their needs and desires. I was glad to see that an alternative interpretation of my directions had emerged. Beau was establishing ownership of this constructive activity.

MARIA: LEONARDO, THE SUPERHERO. Maria was entranced with Leonardo DiCaprio from the movie, *Titanic*. She said, "he's got it!" and Beau added, "that movie rocks!" Maria decided to make Leonardo as the face of her hero because "he is a kind of a hero in the movie; he saved someone from drowning" (see Figure 4 on page 53). This, of course, was a very different interpretation of the term *superhero*.

Figure 3
Beau's Superhero

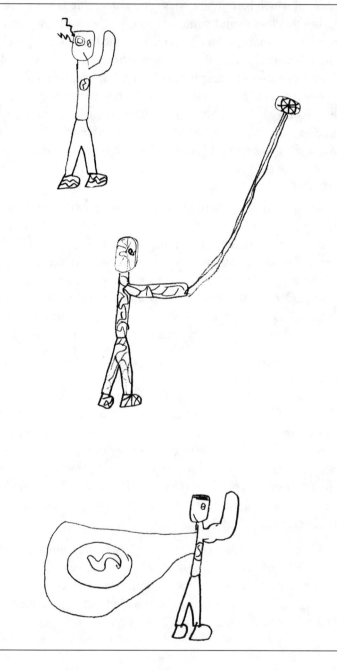

Figure 4
Maria's Superhero

SHIDA: TECHNOLOGICAL SUPERHERO.   Shida, on the other hand, drew from his knowledge of technology-based superheroes, such as Robotech, Transformers, and RoboCop. Shida stated that he chose these superheroes because he liked computers and machines. Interestingly, his depiction of the high-tech superhero (see Figure 5 on page 54) brought nostalgic memories for me of the notebook my brother had filled with the same types of drawings. From my experience, Shida's perfect

Figure 5
Shida's Superhero

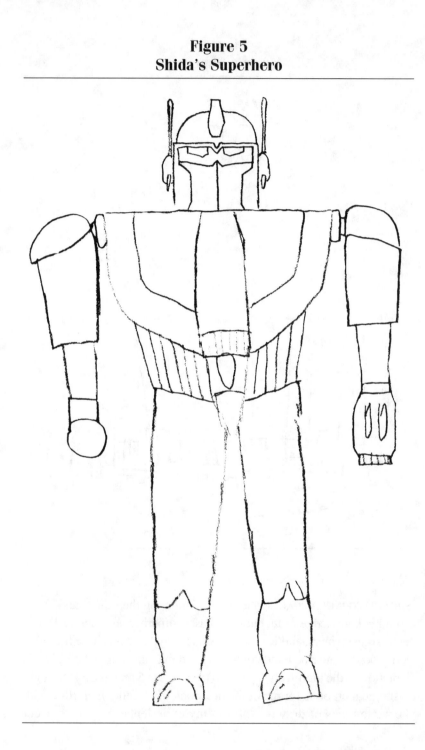

high-tech superhero was a common drawing of superheroes that many Asian male students drew.

CAMERON: THE HUMANITARIAN SUPERHERO.   Cameron's superhero was the perfect example of a conservationist (see Figure 6). He combined features from Flash ("because he's fast and can go around the world in 20 seconds"), Superman ("because he can fly"), Aquaman ("because he can jump into the water and get the whales"), and Spiderman ("because Superman don't have to do all the work"). Cameron had efficiently covered every means possible of getting his superhero to the places he needed to go. Cameron felt that his superhero had to be fast so that he could go "help people and animals."

Figure 6
Cameron's Superhero

In all cases, the children exerted their personal beliefs about what they felt were important goals and powers for their perfect super-heroes to have. In doing so, they allowed me to peek into the window of their fantasies. I learned about who they want to be and how they desire to interact with their world.

Reflections and Extensions

Students' Suggestions for Teachers

I asked both groups of students whether they thought doing a lesson on superheroes and popular culture characters was a good idea. They agreed that it was. They also had several important suggestions "for teachers who want to teach superheroes to their students." They first cautioned that bringing superheroes into classrooms might not be a good idea because "students will get rowdy and hyper" because they will be debating over whether "Superman is better than Batman," and that there might be some "screaming and yelling" involved. However, they also felt that all this might be skillfully avoided by teachers if they would provide guidelines and not allow students to make such comparisons in a "shouting and fighting" voice. They also thought that if "small groups of children will work together they will not get carried away." They all agreed that activities using superheroes and popular culture in classrooms are worthwhile because everyone has fun and, as Cameron said, it is valuable because children can "learn how to save the world." When asked how the other students in the class would react to doing a lesson on superheroes, one student responded that they will be "amazed" that a teacher would do it.

The following is a list of suggestions that classroom teachers might want to consider when introducing popular culture texts in their classrooms. These came from the students I worked with; the wording is my own.

1. Do small-group lessons led by the teacher, or do student-led lessons if students are serious.
2. Avoid encouraging competitive attitudes among students.
3. Allow students to select their own popular culture materials.
4. Try to keep up to date on what students like.

5. Allow students to have fun, but do not let them get out of control.

Some Ideas for Extending the Lesson on Superheroes

As with any kind of lesson on multifaceted topics such as popular culture and media studies, there were many different layers of information about the students that raised questions and issues for me. As educators, we often look to the students we are teaching, or to the participants we are studying, to see what issues and questions will emerge. Listening to students for possible extensions and themes to explore has always been my philosophy of teaching. Thus, it was natural that I would do the same thing with these two groups of students.

Positioning myself as a teacher and researcher, I saw several areas that could be explored using popular culture texts. For example, the appropriateness of studying popular culture with gender as the focus seems to be a natural one. This idea came to me during the lesson as students referred to their superhero as a "he" (including the two female students). Both Pilar and Maria drew male superheroes even though my instruction to them was to draw *themselves*. Pilar drew Zorax for her head, while Maria drew Leonardo DiCaprio. The names of the superheroes they brainstormed were also all male except for Storm. Their gender-skewed responses support what Dyson (1997) found in her study of young students writing about superheroes in their writing workshops. Frustrated with boys taking the key roles of superhero characters, such as the X-Men, in their written plays, some of the girls in Dyson's study took it upon themselves to create their own desirable roles using their own scripts.

In addition to not constructing themselves as female superheroes in their drawings, Pilar and Maria also demonstrated a nonmainstream interpretation of whom they considered to be superheroes. Except for Shida, all the other boys constructed themselves as "traditional" superheroes (for example, Superman, Spiderman, Wolverine). I can only speculate on the implications of these responses and offer my interpretation of them. First, I think superheroes are defined by their muscles, power, and ability to help those who are weaker than themselves (such as women and children). Although as educators we continue to explore ways to equalize the power and representation of children's voices in the classroom context, we have largely ignored the visual representation of images they see and live with as soon as they walk outside the school building. There is an imbalance of gender in superheroes they know, and although a few popular female superheroes (for example, Wonder Woman, Bat Girl, Super Girl) do exist, they are usually characters who have derived from the complementary male superheroes. Rarely do the female superheroes stand on their own.

A Gender-Focused Lesson Extension

The two girls whom I observed in my lesson had to do more work than the boys to reconstruct their superhero identities. That is to say, they were limited by the available resources of female superheroes with whom they might identify. What they eventually constructed were images partially reflecting the mainstream view of gender and partially rejecting it (Leonardo DiCaprio and a relatively unknown, less-popular character, Zorax). This caused me to think about how female students position themselves within the context of various popular culture texts. Certainly they have to do more work than boys in sorting through which images they can "buy into" and which images they can reject because there are fewer direct and transferrable images available to them. Interestingly, none of the boys mentioned or incorporated female superheroes. If we do not open possibilities for both female and male students to see ways of being "the other" (at least symbolically), or provide opportunities to critically discuss these possibilities, they are likely to develop skewed perspectives on gender in their personal and social lives.

The following are some ideas for a lesson that might open such possibilities. Brainstorm with students the names and special powers of female superheroes. Compare this list with another list of male superheroes and their special powers. Discuss differences and similarities between the two lists. Talk about why differences might exist in the number and type of special powers male and female superheroes have. Discuss how these differences might be compensated for or changed.

Another idea for a gender-focused lesson came from observing a fifth-grade teacher in a school in New York City. The teacher constructed a lesson in which the students made "superhero cards." These cards were fashioned after popular baseball cards. Students in the class used the superhero cards to illustrate their understanding of how power worked. They also traded their superhero cards with one another. As an extension of this idea, students might do a gender-focused lesson in which they combine desirable features from different strong female superheroes to make superhero cards.

Personal Themes and What to Do With Them

Uncovering how students are constructing themselves in their real and fantasy worlds is where I see the greatest potential for using popular culture to teach critical media literacy in the classroom. The 30-minute lesson that I did provided Chris with a way to share a deep and private concern he had about death and dying. The simple drawing exercise caused him to make connections with his personal experiences and memories (a family member's death) and to share those thoughts and feelings with his classmates. This is what teachers of writing workshop hope to achieve in their writing activities; that is, to make literacy experiences personal and powerful. The students with whom I worked were able to express and share their private worlds with one another in the form of a pictorial text.

This lesson also spoke to me personally. I realized that I, as the teacher, can prepare the lesson and can anticipate what may happen, but I cannot predict what the students will bring to the lesson. I learned the importance of trusting children, being willing to take the role of the facilitator, and being flexible in allowing the students to shape the lesson.

If I had had more time to work with Chris, I would have wanted to have had a one-on-one conference with him to explore his thinking and feelings further. Based on what I might have learned from that conversation, he and I might have negotiated whether or not the topic was one that he wanted to do an independent project on, such as writing a script or a story for his superhero. This kind of an extension can be a risk-free way for students to explore their fears and desires through imagining themselves as superheroes. Because their picture texts were so diverse and individualistic, each of the children I worked with could have done an independent, exploratory project as an extension lesson.

One final point worth considering is Luke's (1997) cautionary note about developing children's individual voices within a progressive classroom. In her words,

> Teachers need to take seriously and to acknowledge students' different readings of and pleasures derived from popular culture while guarding against potential slippage into a vacuous celebration of individual taste, pleasure, or personal responses.... [T]he postmodern turn to difference and heterogeneity does not mean that "anything goes." What it does mean is that a commitment to social justice principles should guide [a] teacher's work in enabling students to come to their own realizations. (pp. 46–47)

Long before students enter primary school, they have been consumers of popular culture. Even the youngest of these students do not buy into popular culture blindly or without conscious and meaningful intentions. However, they do need to be shown by teachers some different ways of critically examining the assumptions underlying the various popular culture texts that they encounter.

CHAPTER 4

Engaging Upper Elementary Students in Critical Media Literacy: Margaret's Lesson

During my years of teaching elementary school, I packed my curriculum full of educational activities that expanded on my students' interests. It was not uncommon that on any given day, my lesson book would be revised as a result of a group of children having found a chrysalis on the playground or because several students noticed the refraction of light on our classroom wall after a heavy rain. When the children began asking questions about these phenomena, I would rush to get chart paper to jot down their thoughts. Then, we would explore and discover as a class the answers to their innumerable questions. Sometimes these investigations lasted a few days, while at other times topics might become a year-long ongoing study. My students' interests were always the deciding factor in determining the length of the project.

Looking back now, I realize that although I would willingly revamp my day or year to tap into students' academic interests, I never jumped on an opportunity to expand on students' thoughts about the Walt Disney version of the fairy tale *The Little Mermaid* nor did I investigate with them their questions about the controversy of wearing T-shirts to school that portrayed cartoon characters advertising cigarettes and beer. Occasionally, over brown-bag lunches in the cafeteria, I would become involved in their conversations about the strongest cartoon character or the scariest R.L. Stine horror book, but once the bell rang to return to class, those conversations were over. I did not

61

ever record any of their many questions or explore their various positions about these subjects. Honestly, it never even crossed my mind.

But now, exposing myself to these forms of popular culture has made me realize that I missed out on valuable teaching opportunities. And like the sanctioned divergences that I encouraged and allowed for studies that I deemed worthy, students' readings of popular cultural texts seem just as relevant and important an area of learning. So to put this thought process into practice, I decided to teach a critical media literacy lesson with a group of fourth graders.

This chapter is a retelling of my attempts to address the many facets of my learning and teaching critical literacy using student-selected examples of popular music. I have tried to accurately chronicle the steps I took in designing, researching, preparing, and teaching this lesson because it was through this process of reflection and discovery that I was able to develop this idea. As you read this lesson, I encourage you to consider how you would implement or alter these steps to design a lesson using students' popular culture for your own classroom.

Deciding on the Topic

I spent some time doing "kidwatching" (Goodman, 1985) to ascertain the interests of this group before choosing the topic of the lesson. First I observed the students in the classroom. Strictly from this visual perspective, I learned that most of the boys were interested in science fiction and the revival of the *Star Wars* movies as noted by the T-shirts they wore and the books they were reading (a *Star Wars* series by Kevin J. Anderson and Rebecca Moesta), whereas the girls were interested in overalls, T-shirts bearing name brands, and Baby-Sitters Club books. But from this perspective it was difficult to find a common area of interest for boys and girls when I was basing my observations on sight alone.

I changed strategies and attended to the students' social interactions while they were at lunch, on the playground, and in transition between classes. By doing this, I was able to learn about their interests from their conversations. I noticed that they spent a lot of time casually singing songs and talking to one another about music—not their music class at school but about songs that they heard on the radio or on music television. For example, one day as I was walking down the fourth-grade hall, I noticed three girls standing around the water fountain singing a song by Hanson, the popular brother trio band. Then, later in the week, I also noticed that several students had written the names of bands on their daily homework folders as a kind of artwork design. From these observations, I determined that teaching a lesson on critical literacy using music would certainly capture this particular group's interests. Using this information, I thought that I would solicit the students' expertise and preferences in choosing the examples of popular songs around which I would then create a lesson.

Choosing the Examples

When designing this lesson, I wanted to ensure that I would include both the students' pleasures of the examples that were chosen as well as provide opportunities for critical analysis of these examples. Therefore, I originally planned for students to bring their favorite songs to school and use their compact discs (CDs) as the musical examples in the lesson I would teach. But when thinking through this strategy I realized that I could potentially be faced with several issues that might detract from a successful lesson. For instance, using songs from every child would make it too difficult to find a theme to investigate (and the purpose of the lesson was to think critically about music and not necessarily listen to all of the students' musical preferences). Then, I thought that I would have the students form groups and have each group choose a CD to bring to school for the lesson. Using this design would allow students time to discuss their pleasures and come up with a consensus. But then I worried that students might bring in objectionable material that violated school policies. And, using this method still did not address the problem of too many songs without a common theme to explore.

Taking all this information into consideration, I chose to use a survey format to solicit students' input. I thought that this approach would address my key concerns. By providing students the opportunity to share their favorite songs, I could validate their musical preferences and learn about the pleasures that they derived from their song choices. Also, by asking students to describe the song, I would better understand their level of comprehension of the lyrics. Furthermore, by using a survey format, I hoped to find enough group consensus to yield two favorite songs that I could use as examples in the lesson as opposed to having a classroom full of children vying for an opportunity to play their CDs. And, by using the survey format, I thought I would be able to filter any songs or material that might potentially violate school policy.

Before my initial meeting with the students, I drafted the survey for each child to complete. It included spaces to write the titles of three favorite songs, to describe each song, and to explain why the child liked each song (see Figure 7).

Administering the Survey

When I met with the students, I was confident from my observations that I had pinpointed an area of interest that they would want to discuss in the classroom. However, when I told them that I would be teaching a lesson about music, the students' reactions were much different than I anticipated. The students just rolled their eyes and several of them muttered to one another under their breath that they had already been to music that week. At that point, several children began complaining that music was boring and that they were tired of learning how to identify silent notes and keep a steady beat.

Their responses confused me. Reacting to their negative reception, I began to cite examples of my observations of their love of music telling them that I had overheard them discussing music videos and singing songs as they walked down the hallway. They looked stunned and surprised. Finally, one boy spoke up and asked somewhat incredulously, "Oh, you mean like real music? Do you mean you are going to teach a lesson about *real* music? How do you do that?"

Curiously, these students did not consider music learned at school as "real." To them, school music was dull and distinctly separate from music that they listened to outside of school. So when I first used the term *music* to describe the lesson I would be teaching, they immediately associated it with their school music class. But as I recounted examples of their musical interests from my observations, the students clarified the distinction between real music and school music. Once the misunderstanding of the term *music* was elucidated, the students' interests were sparked and they were very willing to share their "real"

Figure 7
Music Survey

Your Name_____

Write the names of your three favorite songs and the artist or band that performs each song.

Song Name   Band/Artist

_____   _____

_____   _____

_____   _____

Describe what you think each song is about.

Song 1: _____

_____

_____

Song 2: _____

_____

_____

Song 3: _____

_____

_____

Why do you like each of these songs?

Song 1: _____

_____

_____

Song 2: _____

_____

_____

Song 3: _____

_____

_____

musical preferences. I explained the survey to them, answered the questions they had, waited for them to complete their surveys, and collected them to take with me. I then used the information on their surveys to choose the songs that I would use as examples in the lesson.

Shuffling through the collected surveys, I realized that this group of children had a variety of musical tastes that spanned a multitude of musical genres. Their favorite songs included alternative radio hits by the band Matchbox 20, softer songs by Mariah Carey, and contemporary Christian rock songs by Michael W. Smith. A few students mentioned classical scores by Beethoven and "oldies" by Van Morrison as well as rap singers and songs. However, when tallying the overall favorites, two bands received the most votes: Puff Daddy and the Family and their song, "I'll Be Missing You," and the Backstreet Boys' song, "As Long as You Love Me." To be quite honest, I was not familiar with either of these bands or their songs, so I knew that I must learn something about them before creating a lesson using these songs as examples.

Researching the Students' Choices

I began my search for information at a local music store. Taking the Puff Daddy and the Family CD from the rap section and the Backstreet Boys CD from the rock/R&B aisle, I sat down at a headset station to listen to the lyrics of the two songs. Looking at the CD covers, I noticed that the bands looked similar. Both groups were comprised of five or six male members, and both CD jackets portrayed the members standing together as a group with serious expressions on their faces. However, the Puff Daddy CD had a sticker on it that read, "Parental Advisory: Explicit Content." I thought about returning the CD to its section and choosing the next highest ranked favorite on the students' survey because I did not want to have to address this issue in the classroom. But then I thought better of it and decided to at least listen to the song the students chose before moving to other options. Listening to the songs, I found neither one objectionable to the school's policy so I bought the CDs. At that point, though, I was still unsure how I was going to set up the lesson. I still did not have enough information about the bands to make any decisions.

Before leaving the store, I asked two young adults who worked there to describe the two bands for me. I thought that by getting feedback from them I would get a better feel for the groups and their music. Both of the employees described Puff Daddy and the Family as an older band for a mature audience but that their song "I'll Be Missing You" had been played on the radio and that it was popular with listeners of all ages. Then they described the Backstreet Boys as a band currently popular with young adolescent audiences. Comparing them to the all male, adolescent bands Menudo and New Kids on the Block, they dubbed the band as "in" now but they would "be history" when the next teen band came along. I wondered how these music buffs knew this information about these band images, and I wondered if these fourth-grade students were aware of the differences as well.

As I looked at the CD jackets later, I noticed that the Puff Daddy CD had an Internet address reference printed on it. So, I put the Backstreet Boys CD into my computer so that I could get a feel for their music while I surfed the Internet for information on Puff Daddy and the Family. To my surprise, when I hit play on my computer's CD drive, my computer screen lit up with fireworks and spotlights as if I were at a concert. There in front of me was an auditorium filled with teenagers screaming and chanting in unison, "Backstreet Boys, Backstreet Boys." After viewing several camera angles of a rowdy and happy crowd, the five Backstreet Boys appeared on the screen and announced that I had bought an "enhanced CD" that would allow me to "enter the Backstreet Boys' world."

"The Boys" then led me through a series of menus and choices where I learned about each band member's background including their favorite foods and their ideal date just by clicking on a button. I watched one of their videos, shopped "virtually" their band paraphernalia, and linked to other Backstreet Boys Web sites. After about an hour of touring with the band via my enhanced CD, I felt well acquainted with the members of the group: Nick, Howie, Brian, A.J., and Kevin. My trek into their world changed my position from that of a Gen-Xer (short for Generation X, a label commonly applied to people born between 1961 and 1980) to that of a screaming adolescent fan. I became part of the audience of cheering fans immersed in learning every bit of trivia that "The Boys" were willing to offer.

Exiting from the unexpected enhanced CD detour, I resumed my Internet search for information on Puff Daddy and the Family. The Internet address printed on the album cover took me to the "Bad Boy, Inc." homepage. I noticed while perusing this site that Puff Daddy and the Family took a much different approach to informing their audience than did the Backstreet Boys. As with the Backstreet Boys CD, I was able to listen to the newest Puff Daddy release by clicking on an icon shaped like a speaker, but I was not offered the same kind of trivia about Puff Daddy that the Backstreet Boys volunteered to their audience. In contrast to how I felt positioned by the teenage mania of the Backstreet Boys' enhanced CD, I read the media text of the Puff Daddy Web site without changing my position at all. I noticed that interacting with this band of artists I presumed to be in their late 20s was natural and enjoyable.

The Puff Daddy and the Family homepage did not offer information about each band member's favorite color and personal clothing styles. Instead, this group set up their Web site as a kind of tribute to the band member Notorious B.I.G. and chronicled the band's time together using pictures and a few short blurbs. I learned that Notorious B.I.G. was shot and killed in a drive-by shooting and the song "I'll Be Missing You" was written in memory of him. Once again I questioned using this CD in the lesson as this song was written in response to an act of violence. However, I decided that since the students chose the song and because the song did not contain any material that violated school policy, I would incorporate it into the lesson and see where the discussion would lead the group. So, to prepare myself to be able to discuss this issue in the classroom, I learned all I could about Notorious B.I.G.'s death and the band members' responses to his death.

Designing the Lesson

Comparing the information about the two bands that I had learned from my search, I was beginning to notice the differences between them that were relayed to me by the music experts at the music store. My first reaction when looking at their CD jackets was to lump them together into a category of male bands that sang popular songs liked by fourth graders; however, after further investigation, I realized they were really quite different by the images that they portrayed to audiences and from the songs that they sang. I decided that I would explore these differences with the students.

My lesson then developed into four components. First, students would engage in a discussion to explore the different aspects of musical pleasure. Second, the students would be guided through an activity of reading the bands' images as portrayed on the CD jackets. Third, students would combine their reading of the CD jackets with the lyrics of the songs to further examine their readings of the bands' images. And fourth, students would form small, self-selected groups to create their own musical bands, to construct their own band images on a CD jacket, and to write their own song that exemplified their band's image.

Thinking about the lesson components, I realized that my participation as the teacher would have to change dependent on the component and the students' understanding of the concepts. So that I would be more cognizant of my role, I defined for myself how I would approach each part of the lesson.

Deciding on My Role as the Teacher

Because the lesson combined pleasures of music, components of analysis, and writing of lyrics, I knew that I would need to shift back and forth among roles of novice, guide, and expert. During the portions of the lesson in which students were more knowledgeable, I would drop back and have them assume the role of expert. By doing this, I hoped that the students would feel comfortable sharing their ideas of the music without any judgments from me. But I also recognized that students would be unfamiliar with concepts of positioning and reading images, so during this part of the lesson I planned to assume the role of a guide. I would guide students through the process but not lead them to any particular answers. I planned to monitor carefully the students' interests and use the information they provided to guide the questions that I would ask. Then, when students created their own bands, I realized I might have to assume roles of an expert, guide, or novice depending on each group's needs.

Teaching the Lesson

As I entered the classroom the following day, I was bombarded by a lively group of fourth-grade girls and boys. The students immediately began asking me if we were going to listen to music in the classroom. They wanted to know which songs were the most popular from the surveys and if we were going to discuss the songs in class. I thought to myself as I plugged in my CD player that the energetic reception I was currently receiving was vastly different from what I had witnessed the day before when I first told the students that we were going to discuss music.

We began the lesson by brainstorming students' answers to several questions that I had written on the board. As the students called out their responses, I wrote on the board. When the students had finished answering the questions, the chalkboard looked like what is shown in Table 2.

While students were sharing their ideas, disagreements would arise among them about the validity of some of their answers. For example, when one child said that an element of a good band was long hair, several children objected. The child then explained that to him long hair was a part of being able to play the guitar and "thrash your head around so that your hair moves with the beat." Another child had said that he liked classical music; this was protested by a fellow

Table 2
Student Responses

What are elements of a good band?	What kinds of music do you like?	Why do you listen to music?	Where do you listen to music?
• Vocals	• Oldies	• To sing along	• In my bedroom
• Instruments	• Pop	• To not be lonely	• On the radio
• Beat	• Jazz	• For the beat	• In my mom's car
• Good meanings of songs	• Classical	• It is something to do	• On television
• Good friends	• Country	• It's fun	• At my friend's house
• Long hair	• Soft Rock	• To get ideas about what to do	
	• Rap		
	• Rock		

student who said that "classical music is only for old people." But then a third child chimed in and stated that her sister in sixth grade liked classical music, so children could like it.

During this sharing and clarifying of ideas, I did not step in to manage the situation. I noticed that the children were able to defend their own beliefs to the satisfaction of others, so I did not need to get involved. However, using their examples, I had the students reflect on the influences of music on their lives. The children concluded that differences among them were acceptable and that musical tastes were based on opinions.

Having established the various musical interests of the class, I shared with the students the results of the survey. Surprisingly, the students, who had just before agreed to disagree about musical preferences, were all excited about the two songs by Puff Daddy and the Family and the Backstreet Boys. I gave each student a packet of papers that included photo copies of these bands' CD jackets and the lyrics to each song. As they flipped through the pages and talked among themselves, I noticed that most children could identify each of the Backstreet Boys by name but made no mention of the individual members of Puff Daddy and the Family.

Students then were asked to share what they liked about each song. Overall, the students had a superficial understanding of the lyrics and liked both songs for the same reasons. According to the students, both songs had "good beats," "sounded good," and had "easy to understand words." Furthermore, they gave literal descriptions of the songs' lyrics. For example, when describing the song "As Long as You Love Me," the students explained that the song was about boyfriends and girlfriends, and they described the song "I'll Be Missing You" as a song "about being friends and missing a friend that is gone."

Only two boys knew the impetus for the song "I'll Be Missing You," and these boys described to the class the drive-by shooting death of Notorious B.I.G. Although I had prepared myself to discuss this tragedy with the students and I was interested in exploring how the children felt about it, the class did not seem affected by it. So, instead of forcing the students to discuss this issue, I reassessed the situation and let the children's interests guide the discussion of the song. It was not that I was uncomfortable talking about it with the students, but it was clear that the students were not as familiar with the band members of Puff Daddy and the Family so the incident was not as meaningful to them. I also think that I had assumed that just because the song was written in response to a violent act the students would want to talk about it, but they really steered clear of the topic. Perhaps this was because they realized that it was a real occurrence as opposed to movie violence, or maybe they just did not know as much about this band. Either way, we did not have a lengthy discussion of violence or the death of Notorious B.I.G.

After discussing the pleasures of the songs, we moved to the second component of the lesson. Having the students turn to the photo copies of the CD jackets, I explained that we were going to read the images of these two bands. To prepare the students for this, I compared reading band images to using pictures in a storybook to better understand the words written on the page. Several students elaborated on this idea explaining that they used pictures in books to understand the part of the story that was not written down. From this description of how to read pictures, students immediately began discussing among themselves their reading of the Backstreet Boys and Puff Daddy and the Family CD jackets. Like my own initial reading in the music store, the students began listing all the commonalities between the bands. They noted that both bands were all male, that not one of them was smiling, that they all looked cool and serious, and that they all stood together like they were friends.

Then I asked the students to read the CD jacket images by contrasting them. At first the students looked unsure about this question that I had posed. One student finally spoke up saying that they were both alike because they were bands. Other students agreed with this boy's statement. They reiterated the similarities between the groups and then sat staring either at me or at the pictures. At that point, I realized I needed to guide them through reading these images in contrast to one another. So I began by asking them to look at the pictures and read each one separately. As the students began to read each CD jacket picture individually, they were able to distinguish differences between the two bands. Again, as they noted differences, I recorded their responses on the board (see Table 3).

After completing the comparison and contrast of the CD jackets, I had the students listen to each song. I was intrigued by the interest that

Table 3
Differences Between Backstreet Boys and
Puff Daddy and the Family

Backstreet Boys	Puff Daddy and the Family
• White	• Black
• Longer hair	• Really short hair
• Younger, just kids—trying to look tough	• Older—tough guys
• Soft rockers. They look like punks in kids' clothes.	• Rap singers so they have to look cool.
• They are acting like they think that they are trying to be cool in a band.	• They're wearing really nice clothes—like businessmen. They look like they know what they are doing.
• It looks like they are standing in an alley and waiting for trouble to come.	• It looks like they really are cool and hanging there with friends.
• They are acting.	• They are serious and real.

they took in my equipment. Before I began playing the songs, the students freely asked me several questions about who owned the CDs, where the CDs were purchased, and how the CD remote control worked. At first I thought that these questions were irrelevant to the lesson, but when putting things into perspective, I realized that these questions were influential to their understanding of me teaching them using "their" music. By answering their questions without brushing over them, I validated the way that these fourth-grade students casually consulted with one another about music. I noted that the during this informal exchange, the lesson was becoming more of a balanced interaction among all of us and less of a teacher-student relationship. We were engaging in more natural conversation than a formalized lesson plan, and the students were very receptive to these differences.

After playing each song, the students compared each song's lyrics to the respective band's image. Samples of the students' reading of the band image, the lyrics, and the combination of the image and lyrics are shown in Tables 4 and 5 on pages 74 and 75.

Combining a band's images that were read from the CD jackets with the lyrics of the songs, the students developed more elaborate responses of the meaning of the songs and formed a more in-depth un-

Table 4
Analysis of Backstreet Boys

What is the image you formed from reading the Backstreet Boys CD jacket?	What is the song "As Long as You Love Me" about?	Compare lyrics to the image of the Backstreet Boys.
• They want you to think that they are cool and cute. • They are studs and cool about things.	• This song is about them loving a girl and they don't care what the girl has done. • They do not care about the girl's past or what she's been through. • As long as you love me I will love you back.	• I am cool so you should like me because I don't care what you did before. • The boys are saying I am cool so you should like me. • This song is about love so they want a girlfriend or something.

derstanding of each band's image. For example, when discussing the lyrics and images separately, the students gave perfunctory answers to the questions without considering the other component as relevant. However, when combining their reading of the band's images with the lyrics, they paid more attention to both the meaning of the song and to the bands' images.

The final component of the lesson, which took the students 2 days to complete, entailed forming fictitious bands, constructing band images, and writing songs to portray the band images. The students were assigned four tasks once they had broken into self-selected groups of two to four students. These tasks included in no certain order: naming the band, creating an overall band image as well as individual images for each band member, writing a song to describe an important part of their band's image, and designing a CD jacket featuring each of the band members.

The students' completed work revealed that the groups developed their band images and song lyrics using a variety of strategies to negotiate among the members of the groups what their band images would be and how they wanted others to read their images. Some of

Table 5
Analysis of Puff Daddy and the Family

What is the image you formed from reading the Puff Daddy and the Family CD jacket?	What is the song "I'll Be Missing You" about?	Compare lyrics to the image of the Puff Daddy and the Family.
• Laid-back guys • Subdued • Hey, we're a group so stay away from us.	• It's about the guy's friend who died. • He misses his friend and he is sad. • They will see each other in heaven. • They believe that their friend is in heaven and they will all be together again.	• They are laid back so they can sing slow and no one will make fun of them. • They can take it. They can take the death of their friend because they are tough. • They look tough but that doesn't mean they are tough so they can sing a song for their friend. • It is like sometimes you see a mean-looking dog coming down the street but then you find out he is not mean...so just because they look tough they do not have to be tough when they sing.

the groups readily drew from the class discussion of the Backstreet Boys and Puff Daddy and the Family, modeling themselves after one of the bands discussed and using that image to write their songs. Other groups combined portions of the two bands' images to come up with their preliminary image, then elaborated on this image by drawing from their own ideas to complete their identities. Still other groups constructed their images based on popular culture not discussed during the lesson. The work of the groups who named their bands,

CARD, Duel, and Gemini's, exemplifies three different approaches taken to demonstrate students' understanding of forming and reading images and writing songs to portray their literate understanding of reading popular cultural texts.

CARD

Creating their band name from the first letter of each of their names, CARD (Clay, Andrew, Reed, and Dustin) developed their band's persona based on their reading of the Puff Daddy and the Family CD jacket. They decided that as a group their image would be

Figure 8
CARD's CD Jacket Image

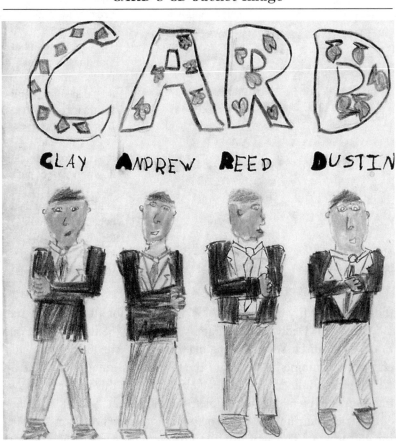

"four guys that are being cool like the guys from Puff Daddy." Like Puff Daddy and the Family, they represented themselves in identical suits and ties because they were "all friends and liked the same styles" (see Figure 8). And they all chose a "cool band image" except for Dustin who identified himself as "sweet."

Although dressed in suits like Puff Daddy and the Family, CARD also used other resources to construct their band image. When asked to read their CD jacket image, they described the different components that were important to them. Their crossed arms, according to Andrew, were based on the way these four boys usually folded their arms before they gave one another a handshake. He explained, "It is like something that we just made up. It is just cool to do that. It is just for friends to do to one another." The stance assumed by each boy originated from watching music television. As Dustin pointed out, "We are just standing like that because we saw it on TV."

Using the melody from Puff Daddy and the Family's hit "I'll Be Missing You," CARD decided as "cool and sweet guys" that they would write a song about a relationship between two people. As Dustin explained, "Give Me Time to Think" is a song about a "boy not knowing if he likes his girlfriend so he is saying that he needs time to think about it. He has to think about if he really wants to be with her or not his whole life. He is deciding between marriage and like staying single" (see Figure 9 on page 78).

Discussing their band image with the lyrics to "Give Me Time to Think," the boys explained that they were cool guys. Pointing to the cocked heads and youthful grins, Reed explained, "you can see that we are all sort of smiling and it kind of looks like we are thinking about something." And Clay added that their CD jacket and their lyrics described how they wanted others to know "about how you need to make your own decisions and stuff like that."

Although none of these 9- and 10-year-old boys had ever experienced having a girlfriend much less making a decision about marriage, they said that they composed the lyrics based on their knowledge of other popular songs and videos. Acknowledging that "sometimes the songs are just there just to listen to…[b]ut sometimes they are there for a point," the members of CARD felt that their song would tell an audience of listeners that "if you really like a girl then just go with it and if you don't then don't go with it. It is basically

Figure 9
CARD's Song "Give Me Time to Think"

Chorus: "Time To Think"
Give me time to think
I can't make up my mind
Somebody tell my
I would rather die
If you do not love me
Then just tell me why
I don't know what to do
Should I spend my life with you
But its really up to you

I remember you
As a dream come true
I really loved you
I hope you loved me too
So that dream is coming true
If you'd just be mine
I'll love you for all time
Why won't you just be mine
I miss you all the time
So just be mine

Chorus: —

just make your own decisions and stuff and don't let other people choose it for you."

Duel

Whit and J.T., the band members of Duel, took a different approach to forming their band image. Unlike the singular approach that CARD used to emulate the identity of Puff Daddy and the Family, Duel decided to combine parts of the images of the Backstreet Boys and Puff Daddy and the Family to develop their own image that was

Figure 10
Duel's CD Jacket Image

"tough like Puff Daddy and cool like the Backstreet Boys." But their images of tough and cool differed from the tough and cool images depicted on the CD jackets of the Backstreet Boys and Puff Daddy and the Family. To illustrate their own understanding of tough and cool, they drew themselves dressed in blue jeans and T-shirts and wearing sunglasses, with one of them wearing a medallion chain (see Figure 10 on the previous page).

Duel also used their image to write their song, "I'm Different" (see Figure 11). Describing themselves as "laid back and relaxed, soft and cool," J.T. and Whit recounted that they had first written a song they titled "The Way of Love" because "most songs are about love and stuff." They said that their song was about a "guy who lost his girlfriend and

Figure 11
Duel's Song "I'm Different"

I'm Different

As I walk down the street I see what
I can see, seen blacks seen white
see'n boys, see'n girls, see'n all the
people that I can see I just a difference
everyday we have fun and play every day
we get rough and cold all the people take a
path sometimes people feel the rath
            Chorus:
I'm different, yeah, I'm just cool
and different, that's just the way I am,
I'm so different

Some people are small or tall somtimes
we're sad or glad in away we have a
difference, if all emotions were the same
there'd be some personali ter may be just a
reality

he wants her back but he does not know how," but when they finished the song they were not satisfied with it "because it was the same thing over and over." They decided that they wanted to do something unique so they started over and composed a new song about differences in people. Whit explained that their song "I'm Different" is about "a black man and he is walking down the street and he is thinking about all of the people that he passes on the street and how everybody looks different. Like nobody is exactly the same and that is cool."

Asserting their own differences in their song, Whit and J.T., both small boys in their class, felt it important to note that differences were all right. They rationalized that "people listen to songs and they learn things," so by listening to their song "people would all think about being treated equally...[they] would not have to worry about their differences, their color, or what country that they came from. So everybody can be the same, you know, like the same because you are different. They could learn that it is okay to just be you...so like when you sing a song about being different then people will like listen to it and think about it."

Gemini's

Dubbing themselves Gemini's, Amanda, Casey, Elizabeth, and Iris described their group image as "nice, weird, funny, and talented." Interestingly, this group, unlike CARD and Duel who used the Backstreet Boys and Puff Daddy and the Family images, chose to compose their image based on themselves as fourth-grade girls "without being too fancy or looking too famous." These four girls designed their CD jacket to resemble each of them as she was dressed that day at school. But when they had completed their drawing they conferred and decided to "jazz it up a little," so they added some lightning bolts to their clothing and wrote the name Gemini's in cursive (see Figure 12 on page 82).

Although Gemini's consciously constructed their band image based on their own identities and ideas of a rock band, they used their understanding of popular culture to develop the idea for their song "Green, Blue, White" (see Figure 13 on page 83). This song that details these girls' dream of a perfect wedding day developed from their understanding that "bands sing a lot about love and boyfriends and girlfriends, like the Backstreet Boys sang about loving a girl and Puff Daddy sang about loving his friend."

Figure 12
The Gemini's CD Jacket Image

Like the members of CARD, the girls in Gemini's had never actually experienced the concepts about which they wrote their song, yet they were able to construct an elaborate account of their notion of a perfect wedding. Casey explained that the group used information that they had learned "from watching movies and books and stuff like that" to form their ideas about the perfect wedding. When describing the song, Iris said, "It is like what we dreamed of what it would be like on our wedding day, who we're going to get married to, what the wedding would be like. It would have perfect green grass, a perfect blue sky." Amanda added that the girl getting married "only trusts the man she will marry" and Elizabeth noted that "It's like a mess because all

Figure 13
The Gemini's Song "Green, Blue, White"

Green, Blue, White

Green Grass, Blue Skies, My wedding dress,
the sun and the moon and my lipstick
CHORUS

It's just a red lipstick and a white
wedding dress sounds familiar sounds
like a mess your the only one I trust and
love you are the above you are the above

Green grass, Blue skies, My wedding dress
the sun and the moon and my mascara
CHORUS

Green as the grass as blue as
the sky and ohhh the kiss
oooooo ——

of the stuff is everywhere, like all of these wedding presents and like all of this wrapping paper. And everything has to be like all perfect for the wedding and it is really hard to do all that." When asked what listeners would learn from their song, the Gemini's unanimously agreed that if an audience listened to the words, "they would learn about weddings and love and girls."

Concluding Thoughts

The completed work by the bands demonstrated their understanding of reading popular cultural images and lyrics and constructing themselves using this process. The students incorporated both what they learned from the lesson as well as other media texts not discussed in class in order to form their images. Furthermore, these students, although all part of the same audience during the lesson, exerted their own personal beliefs to develop interesting and thought-provoking images that were unique. And, by allowing students time to discuss and explain their rationale for their image formation and song lyrics, I learned about their active construction of the interplay of these components on their reading of popular culture.

CHAPTER 5

Engaging Middle School Students in Critical Media Literacy: Donna's Lesson

Last year when I finally gave away my collection of eight-track tapes to a local organization that collects memorabilia for resale to benefit local charitable groups, I knew an end of an era had come. I had been holding on to the tapes of Neil Diamond, Meatloaf, Chicago, Joan Baez, Willie Nelson, and the Moody Blues partly for nostalgic reasons but also for the simple fact that my eight-track tape player still worked quite well. However, as it became increasingly difficult to find new albums on eight-tracks, I kept vowing that I would drive to the local audio and video store and purchase a CD player. The event that actually precipitated my purchase of a portable CD player was the critical media lesson I am about to describe.

Background on the Lesson

For some time, I have been interested in critical theory (see Chapter 7) as it is applied to media literacy. The opportunity to try a critical media literacy lesson using popular culture texts with Dera Weaver's class of eighth graders would give me a chance to see for myself if the theory worked as well in practice as it did on paper. Specifically, I was interested in introducing her students to an adaptation of a strategy called Masquerade (Cohen, 1998). This strategy, which takes into account some of the elements of critical theory, also involves parody and a playful juxtaposition of disparate elements in ways that disrupt a commonsense flow of meaning. Strategies that help us disrupt what seems natural or commonsensical to our usual way of thinking about things make it possible to read against the grain—that is, to examine taken-for-granted ideas so that we are open to new ways of seeing or thinking.

For example, in Figure 14 any meaning we might typically attribute to the image of the German Shepherd as a breed of dog is more than likely going to be disrupted by the red-and-white Santa Claus hats that my two dogs, Quandra and Deidre, are wearing. This picture can be read in one of several contexts. For instance, are they the kind of German Shepherds you have read about in the paper who attack neighborhood children or assist the police in tracking down hardened criminals? Or, are they less threatening because they permitted us to photograph them in ridiculous-looking hats? Why is the "otherness" we glimpse in this picture of two dogs from a well-known, often feared breed so compelling an object of study? Who is the "real" Quandra? Who is the "real" Deidre? Does this photo reinforce or subvert the stereotype you have when you think of German Shepherds? And what does the notion of "otherness" have to do with all this?

To understand "otherness" is to first challenge the assumption that we can ever separate ourselves from those we would call "Other." The Other is always present in the images we hold of ourselves—images that we construct with certain audiences in mind. According to Cohen (1998), this relationship between self and Other is like a performance:

> We learn how to pose for the camera at an early age and those poses often stay with us all our adult lives, becoming part of our second nature; and in that sense we perform our identity for and by means of the Other. At the same time, the Other can also function as that part of our selves which has become foreign to us, but which is nevertheless present in our dreams, our fantasies and indeed in much of our waking life as the subject we secretly hope to become, or once believed we were. (p. 167)

Taking this view of the inseparability of self and Other as my starting point in designing the lesson that follows, I wanted to introduce the students in Dera's class to an alternative reading of some of the popular culture texts associated with the popular musicians, the Spice Girls and Natalie Imbruglia. Specifically, I was interested in

Figure 14
Challenging the Image of the German Shepherd

finding out whether this group of eighth graders would be able to use my adaptation of Cohen's (1998) Masquerade strategy to unpack, or question, the underlying assumptions of some of the messages delivered by the lyrics from the albums *Spiceworld* and *Left of the Middle*. I also was interested in helping this group of students discover some things about themselves as the audience for these two CDs.

Designing the Lesson

Unlike Jennifer and Margaret, I did not start with the students' interests. That is, I did not ask them to name the bands, solo artists, pop stars, and the like who were their favorites. I made this decision after talking with Dera. She and I knew one another well from having worked together on a number of research projects in the past. Most recently we had coauthored (Weaver & Alvermann, in press) a chapter on teaching middle school students to read their assigned textbooks from a critical perspective. Dera believed, and I concurred, that asking young adolescents in a group setting to come to consensus on what they liked in the way of music (or would even agree to listen to) was a dangerous proposition. Individuals' feelings were bound to get hurt, and the more sensitive ones were likely not to participate in the lesson. Consequently, we decided that I would choose two CDs: one would be the Spice Girls' newest album, *Spiceworld*; the other would be at the suggestion of a knowledgeable young clerk who worked at the music store.

We made this decision because Dera knew that the Spice Girls were held in contempt by most of her eighth graders. Yet, she also knew that at the previous week's school dance, a group of her eighth-grade girls had jumped up on the stage to do a Spice Girls' routine while listening to one of the songs from *Spiceworld*. The parody fit well with the strategy I would be introducing. Moreover, we thought that having an album chosen by a person who worked at a music store that was frequented by young people similar to Dera's group would likely be viewed as a positive move. It was also a way that Dera and I could avoid coming on as the arbiters of what was considered "cool" by this age group.

As agreed upon, I went to the music store in search of the second album, one that most likely would be acceptable to this group of eighth graders. Upon entering the dimly lit store, I was met by a young male clerk who listened as I described what I wanted to buy and why I needed it. He asked what I considered to be several good questions about the group before suggesting that I purchase Natalie Imbruglia's *Left of the Middle*. Little did I know at the time that his questions, which the students later wanted to know, would lead to one of the more interesting parts of the lesson—a point to which I will return.

I also purchased *Spice World: The Official Book of the Movie* (Spice Girls, 1997), which is a 96-page color photo essay that chronicles a busy week in the five pop stars' lives and claims to reveal the real-life characters behind their stage nicknames—Ginger, Sporty,

Posh, Baby, and Scary. If truth be known, the book was for me. I needed some background information, and I needed it quickly. As luck would have it, Margaret saw Natalie Imbruglia's picture on the cover of the June 1998 issue of *Spin* and brought the accompanying article (France, 1998) to me. Jennifer also brought in a short piece on Natalie Imbruglia from *Time*, which billed her as Britain's "hottest export since the Spice Girls" (Thigpen, 1998, p. 223). That clinched it. I knew I had the right pair of CDs. With lyrics, book, and articles in hand, I set about creating the materials that I would need for the lesson.

I felt that any success I would have with Cohen's (1998) strategy depended largely on my ability to plan a lesson that would juxtapose the disparate elements in the messages delivered by the Spice Girls and Natalie Imbruglia. This juxtaposition had to accomplish two things: First, it had to disrupt what seemed commonsensical or natural about the way the pop stars positioned their audience, and second, it had to provoke a lively discussion among the eighth graders. Complicating matters somewhat was the fact I had only one class period of approximately 50 minutes to accomplish my objective, and I did not know the students. However, after many years of traveling throughout the United States doing short demonstration lessons on study strategies with groups of students I had not met previously, I felt prepared for this latest challenge (though admittedly, I knew a lot more about study strategies than I did about the Spice Girls and Natalie Imbruglia). In the end, I decided on an individual pencil and paper warm-up activity followed by a whole-class discussion. There were only 15 students in Dera's language arts class, a factor that figured prominently in my decision to try a large-group discussion.

Creating the Materials

The pencil and paper warm-up activity (see example in Figure 15 on page 90) consisted of four questions to be answered by the students after they had (a) listened to the lyrics of "Spice Up Your Life" by the Spice Girls and "Torn" by Natalie Imbruglia (the first song on each CD); and (b) completed reading the back cover of the *Spice World* book (Figure 16 on page 91) and two short-captioned pictures from the *Spin* article on Natalie Imbruglia (Figures 17 and 18 on pages 92 and 93). The four questions, which were the same for Natalie

Figure 15
Pencil and Paper Warm-Up Activity

Your Name _____

Please read the back cover of *Spice World* by the Spice Girls and then answer these questions:

1. What is the *visual image* of the Spice Girls saying?

2. What *message* is the printed text trying to get across?

3. Do *you*, personally, agree with the message? Why or why not?

4. How could you resist (or argue with) the message, if you wanted to do so?

Imbruglia as for the Spice Girls (shown in Figure 15), focused on the messages (both textual and image-based) that the recording stars seemed to want to convey to their audience. Two of the four questions tapped the students' responses to those messages by asking them if they personally agreed (why or why not), and how they might resist (or argue with) the messages if they chose to do so.

The lyrics from "Spice Up Your Life" consist of directions for performing one of the Spice Girls' dance routines. By moon-walking the fox-trot, for example, and entreating listeners to engage in hip

Figure 16
Back Cover of *Spice World*

From *Spice World: The Official Book of the Movie* by Five Girls Ltd. Copyright ©1997 by Five Girls Ltd. Reprinted by permission of Crown Publishers, Inc.

Figure 17
Natalie Imbruglia Photo and Caption

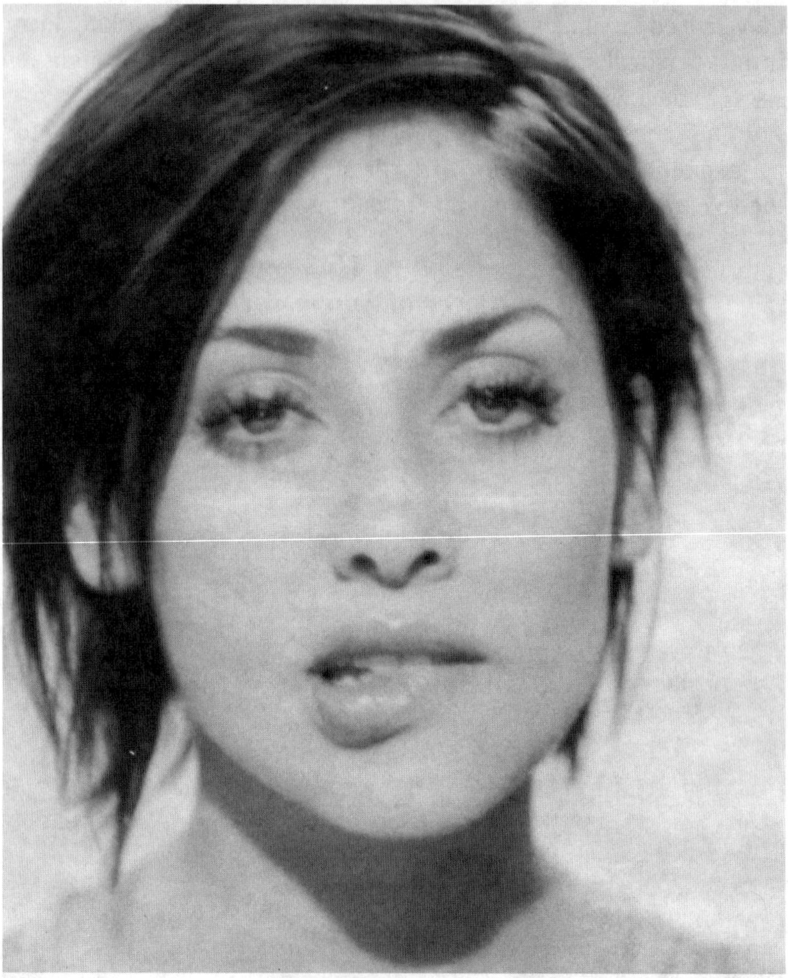

The triumph of "Torn" proves that, if there is one thing that teenage girls love, it's knowing that pretty girls get their hearts stomped on too.

Photographer: Elfie Semotan. Photo used with permission.

shaking, the Spice Girls hope, as the title of the song suggests, to spice up their audiences' lives.

Juxtaposed to this song, Natalie Imbruglia's lyrics seem angst-ridden. In "Torn," Imbruglia laments a failed relationship that left her

Figure 18
Natalie Imbruglia Photo and Caption

"The only thing I'm lacking is experience, and unfortunately I'm going to have to gain it in public. But better this way than never having success at all."

Photographer: Elfie Semotan. Photo used with permission.

feeling used. Yet the disparate messages are meant to speak to an adolescent audience in ways that blur the boundaries between self and Others. The questions in the warm-up activity were designed to elicit the eighth graders' awareness of the artists' attempts to blur such boundaries and also to encourage the students to imagine different positions available to them as they read to unpack some of the assumptions behind the messages.

Engaging the Students

I arrived at the school where Dera teaches about 10 minutes early, as she had suggested I do. Taking a seat at an empty table in the atrium that opens on to the eighth-grade wing and its four homerooms, I felt conspicuous with my new CD boombox in hand and copies of *Spice World* and *Spin* under my arm. However, when the bell rang for classes to pass, the students paid little or no attention to my presence as they exchanged one set of books for another at their bookbag racks. I joined the group headed into Dera's room. She introduced me to the class as someone from the University of Georgia who was interested in learning about their responses to some messages that certain recording artists in the music industry like to convey to audiences.

I began the lesson by asking the students to listen to "Spice Up Your Life" and "Torn." As I passed out the set of questions and readings that accompanied each CD, I explained that their responses to these materials would provide an entry point into the whole-class discussion that would follow. While the students wrote, Dera took notes, which she later gave to me. At one point in her notes, she remarked, "I'm impressed with how seriously they're writing." With music from the two CDs playing in the background, the students thought and wrote for about 15 minutes. A few asked me to clarify one or more of the questions.

As I moved around the room, I recalled several things that Dera had told me about the students when we first discussed the possibility of my doing a critical media literacy lesson with them. All were there because their parents had opted for a private school education. Of the nine boys and six girls, only one (a male) was African American; the others were of European American background. All came from middle-class homes, and most had known one another for several years prior to entering Dera's class. According to Dera, these students liked to talk and would enter willingly into a discussion in which they were asked to voice their own opinions.

Indeed, a lively and informative discussion did follow. For the last 35 minutes of the class period, the students shared their thinking about the two CDs and their interpretation of the messages that the Spice Girls and Natalie Imbruglia were attempting to convey to them as the audience. Initially, the discussion centered around the questions the students had been asked to consider. Generally, the class was critical of the Spice Girls, seeing them as artificial, mercenary, and inappropriate role models for young adolescent girls. Alex's comments in Figure 19

Figure 19
Alex's Responses to the Spice Girls

Your Name ___Alex___

Please read the back cover of Spice World by the Spice Girls and then answer these questions:

1. What is the visual image of the Spice Girls saying?

The spice girls definitely appeal to girls because all the girls want to look & live like them. They always seem like they are having fun. They ~~don't~~ ~~promote~~ The spice girls look very artificial & appeal to boys for their looks.

2. What message is the printed text trying to get across?

The promote "girl power" & don't ever seem to do anything but hang around.

3. Do you, personally, agree with the message? Why or why not?

No, "girl power" is fun to make fun of, but I don't think anyone really takes them seriously. They act like little girls.

4. How could you resist (or argue with) the message, if you wanted to do so?

Just ignore them & they'll go away ; they can't last to much longer.

Table 6
Responses to Questions 1–4 About the Spice Girls

Note: Students' original spellings and grammar have been retained.

Visual Image	Message of Printed Text	Personally Agree? Why/Why Not	How Might You Resist?
It says that they do every-thing. That they're great & that they can do everything.	That they are so good, every-body wants to hear, read, & watch them.	No, I don't. It makes people not only jealous but also low-ers they're self esteem be-cause they're not as pretty.	By paying no attention and just not care what they think if you feel that way.
The pictures of them have so much makeup that they're pretty & they look at life as a game.	The text is saying they are a lot different when they are just by themselves and not on camera.	Yes, every actor/actress is dif-ferent in their personal life that they are at big events.	I think that kids might want to be more like the spice girls and considering the spice girls dress and act different, this in-fluence might be negative.
They are great girls that have no problems and they think they are great. The pic-tures might also be trying to show that looks of the spice girls. So the person seeing the picture may read on.	It says it's a must for all superspicers, so if you don't buy it you aren't a true spice girls fan.	No I dont. You could be a big spice girls fan and not care too much for the movie, or what they did in their trailors. A person could still have all of their albums.	Just think about all the other ways I could spend my money...
...that women should be heard around the world.	That there are more things to them than what you see on stage. They do a lot of things behind the scenes and no one knows about and you can hear about it in a book.	No, I don't think that anyone needs to know about what they do behind the scenes and in their trailers.	I would say that it's just a money making gimick to get people to buy these products. ...not listen to them.
	...trying to get the reader(s) excited, about whats in this book so that they will read on.		I would argue with their im-age because it is not how they truly are.

(continued)

Table 6
Responses to Questions 1–4 About the Spice Girls (continued)

Visual Image	Message of Printed Text	Personally Agree? Why/Why Not	How Might You Resist?
They are pretty young & have chatchy tunes. For the guyes they wear lots of short tight stuff. For girls they have the fun tunes & like little girls want to grow up & be like them.	If you like the Spice Girls you should buy their book.	No, I do not agree with the message because the message wants you to buy the book, and I do not want to.	Just ignore them & they'll go away; they can't last to much longer.
...It's an inside look at there lives behind the scenes.	...you get to see their "behind the scenes action."	No, I think they are trying to make money...	I don't buy their stuff, and I refused to go to their movie.
They are trying to show that they are average people.	That they want us (the buyer) to read about what they thought of there movie.	No. They just out there to make this book to try to trap young kids into worshiping them.	I can tell myself that I'm perfect the way I am.
...it looks like they are just trying to be seen. They are awful.	...to show the public that they are real people in real life behind all the mics and cameras.	No, because they continuously are trying to sell something few want to buy, just like Hanson.	If I were to say they always act the same as we see on t.v.
The image that I get is that they are 5 girls that want to be the image of the perfect girls and they want to promote girl power.	To buy their stupid book. It is purly to get little kids to think it is something cool to read their book.	Yes, I think it is neat that they are showing who they really are behind the glamour.	Not go off and buy their book because it is a waste of money.
		No it is stupid. There is no reason why I want to learn about Spice and Girl power.	I will tell myself that the Spice Girls are con artists and I don't like their music.
			That it is false & a trap & that the Spice Girls probly didn't even write it.

(continued)

Table 6
Responses to Questions 1–4 About the Spice Girls (continued)

Visual Image	Message of Printed Text	Personally Agree? Why/Why Not	How Might You Resist?
...they are trying to potray a sexy and enthusiastic image.	The book contains a whole bunch of information on the Spice Girls and what they thought of what they did and even one of their set diaries. They wanted you to buy it and they gave you a better idea of what was in it.	Yes, they mention something about "If you wanted to know this then this is the book for you and you should read it."	
The spice girls definitely appeal to girls because all the girls want to look & live like them. They always seem like they are having fun. The spice girls look very artificial & appeal to boys for their looks.	It is talking about their movie and basically who they are.	I kind of agree with their image but the way they are conveying it is not right.	
It's telling girls to have their own identity and that's a good idea. But, they also dress like hookers, so its sort of a mixed message	...one of their messages is that girls "rule." They also try to pull themselves off as tough.	I sort of agree but I think they are too clone up. They try to pass a message as "be yourself" but they have completely been molded into what they producers want them to be.	
	The promote "girl power" & don't ever seem to do anything but hang around. The text is mostly advertising fun: how much fun they had on the set... It's also advertising the movie in a major way.	No, "girl power" is fun to make fun of, but I don't think anyone really takes them seriously. They act like little girls. No! The Spice Girls give such mixed messages and –disgust me.	

summarize fairly well what the class thought about the Spice Girls and *Spiceworld's* message.

Yet, there were some students who thought the Spice Girls' message had an additional layer of meaning. For example, Amy argued that "It's telling girls to have their own identity and that's a good idea. But they also dress like hookers, so its [sic] sort of a mixed message." Pete brought to the class's attention "...that women should be heard around the world." However, Susan's response to Amy and Pete suggested that she saw the irony in the disparate messages that the Spice Girls and Natalie Imbruglia were sending. For example, Susan wanted to know why they both "talked about 'girl power' when all their songs are about guys." And Lisa saw through a veneer that troubled her. She was annoyed that the Spice Girls "didn't get together because of their music, but because they answered an advertisement." To her, this betrayed their attempt to come off as "really good friends" in the movie, *Spice World*. Other comments that formed the basis of the students' conversation about the Spice Girls are listed in Table 6 on pages 96–98.

Overall, the class was more positive toward the person and lyrics of Natalie Imbruglia than they were to the Spice Girls. Several students contributed points to the discussion that indicated they were cognizant of being positioned differently when they listened to the two CDs. Whereas the Spice Girls played up the "pretty girls can get whatever they want" theme, Natalie Imbruglia told it more like "it really is." Susan summarized several of her classmates' responses by noting that "even pretty girls get dumped." Others, however, sensed a more negative image. For example, Rita thought that Natalie Imbruglia was perhaps a bit too carefree, suggesting that Imbruglia thought "life was something to breeze through," and Pete interpreted her message as being a warning that "if you take your chances with a relationship, your heart will be stomped on." Still others chose not to take personally any of the positions Imbruglia's lyrics offered. Instead, they generalized to society at large and spoke of her message as pertaining to someone "out there" but not to them specifically. Lisa's responses in Figure 20 on page 100 are representative of those students' comments.

Although the lyrics from "Torn" may have subverted the stereotype that pretty girls get whatever they want in life, the images of Natalie Imbruglia in *Spin* disrupted this message in the eyes of some of the students. Judy, for instance, noted that the magazine just made

Figure 20
Lisa's Responses to Natalie Imbruglia

Your Name Lisa

Please read the two-page handout on **Natalie Imbruglia** and then answer these questions:

1. What are these <u>visual images</u> of Natalie Imbruglia saying?

She is saying that looks aren't everything, and ~~its~~ although society may not support this, we need to realize it.

2. What <u>message</u> is the printed text trying to get across?

Society puts so much imphasis of looks these days, but in the end, we realize looks and being pretty is not ~~th~~ important.

3. Do <u>you</u>, personally, agree with the message? Why or why not?

I agree because I think it is sad when teenage are anorexic ~~an~~ because they think if they are thin and pretty, it will be the end of their problem If only they realized that their problems are the same no matter how they look.

4. How could you resist (or argue with) the message, if you wanted to do so?

You could say that this is proving there is too much compitition in todays world.

a pretty girl with a pout on her face look sad. Although the discussion did not turn to an analysis of Judy's comments, in retrospect I think this would have been an opportune time to open the possibility that Natalie Imbruglia was merely performing her identity for, and by means of, her audience. Judy's insight certainly hinted at her understanding of that possibility. Similarly, Amy's statement that "girls like to be able to identify with (perhaps) someone who is famous and pretty" suggested that she was well aware of the fact that the Other is always present in the images we hold of ourselves.

An analysis of the students' responses to why they agreed or disagreed with the message of "Torn" and the media's representation of Natalie Imbruglia (see Table 7 on pages 102–104) suggested that they were ambivalent toward her and *Spin*'s attempt to position her in a way that blurred the boundaries between performer and audience. Although the majority of the eighth graders were ready to give Imbruglia and her music a chance at being seriously considered, at least one (a male student) was adamant in his refusal to accept any part of the message. To Pete's way of thinking, Natalie Imbruglia was "very stereotypical because she may have had a bad experience with men, [but] that doesn't mean everyone will."

Interesting as this first part of the discussion was, the more telling comments came in response to Alex's question to me: "How did you know to pick Natalie Imbruglia's CD?" My answer prompted a flurry of reactions, most of which showed that the students were indeed able to unpack what seemed commonsensical or natural about the store clerk's assessment of their likes in popular music. The clerk's questions to me had focused on what type of students would be listening to the CDs I intended to purchase. He wanted to know their age, race, and family's socioeconomic status. He also inquired about the type of school they attended. When he learned that they were mostly middle-class white adolescents who attended a private school, he headed directly for the Natalie Imbruglia section of the display counter. Sharing this information with the class was not something I had intended to do when planning the lesson. However, Alex's interest in determining how I had decided on the CD seemed reasonable enough to me. And, if the truth be told, his question caught me off guard. In retrospect, I am pleased that I did come clean with the students. After all, I had expected them to be direct in their answers to my questions; in my mind, I owed them the same respect.

The students' response to the store clerk's assessment of them as a potential audience was predictable. In short, the situation infuriated Lisa. She retorted, "I don't think who your parents are has anything to do with what you listen to." Charles concurred, adding, "Your parents don't really have much to do with what music you listen to."

Table 7
Responses to Questions 1–4 About Natalie Imbruglia

Note: Students' original spellings and grammar have been retained.

Visual Image	Message of Printed Text	Personally Agree? Why/Why Not	How Might You Resist?
...all people, no matter who they are or how they look will get hurt sooner or later.	That she's young and isn't really trained in the ways of the world.	Yes, because at some point everyone gets hurt in some way.	My choice is to ignore it. I really don't mind.
...looks aren't everything, and although society may not support this, we need to realize it.	Society puts so much imphasis of looks these days, but in the end, we realize looks and being pretty is not important.	...it is sad when teenagers are anorexic because they think if they are thin and pretty, it will be the end of their problems.	I could argue with the message by saying "Well, the pretty girls don't dumped as often."
She is a little messed up. She looks high.	To buy that CD if you want some good wierd music.	Yes, I like the wierd music.	Try not to spend all of your time worrying that people like you or not and concentrate on more important things.
The first picture conveys a soft image of a girl and then the second one is kind of a little more harsh.	...you aren't the only one who has felt bad about something.	Yes, I do agree that everyone will exprience these things and when you do exprience these things it will be imbarrising but it will be better than never expirincing it.	You could argue with message if you believe that nobody can get hurt as long as they have money.
...to show a pretty girl who looks sad or depressed. In the second picture she seems a bit angry or stressed.	...every girl expriencs heart break too. Even when you think that a girl has everything going for her, things will go wrong.	Yes, I agree. Everyone is going to get their heart broken.	She is young, and in-experienced, and sure doesn't know what she's talking about. All she wants is to make money.
	...despite your looks you too will have problems....shows that success comes with experience.	Yes, it's always nice to look good but what really matters is your personality.	

(continued)

Table 7
Responses to Questions 1–4 About Natalie Imbruglia (continued)

Visual Image	Message of Printed Text	Personally Agree? Why/Why Not	How Might You Resist?
The first picture looks like Natalie Imbruglia looks like she has something to say but is biting her lip. The second picture shows Natalie Imbruglia in a "strong" position, she is gritting her teeth & looks more agressive. The pictures are opposites.	The message appeals more to girls because it talks about girls who are pretty, all people want to be attractive. It also tells how its not a perfect life being pretty & tells people to be happy with who they are.	I think having one prominent person who, talks about heartbreak, does help girls understand that this happens to everyone.	Well for the thing about the pretty girl is putting to much imphasis on looks which anoyes me. I like her music & don't necisarily think she meant for it to be about looks but just feelings.
An angry image. More of an independent, wild look. She's sort of disheveled, too, even though she's pretty.	That girls like to be able to identify with (perhaps) someone who is famous and pretty because she has also been hurt.	Yes & No. I don't want to breeze through life. To me life is not a game. Sometimes you take it serious & sometimes you don't have to. If Natalie wants to be carefree, I won't stop her.	Think that the world is a perfect place and that pretty people couldn't possibly be hurt. ...say that this is proving there is too much compitition in today's world.
...like she's not sure of something. She looks a bit carefree.	That life may be something to breeze through.	Yes, everybody has a rough time in their life. Everyone gets dumped at least one-time in their life. Everyone has a bumpy ride in one part of their life.	That is might be bad to listen to that type of music. It could mess me up like it.
The first picture looks like she is thinking about something because of the blank expression and her lip. In the second picture she looks like she is mad about something.	The message is that even the best-looking girls don't have a perfect life, they to get hurt.		You could argue with the message by saying that not everyone experinces these things. *(continued)*

Table 7
Responses to Questions 1–4 About Natalie Imbruglia (continued)

Visual Image	Message of Printed Text	Personally Agree? Why/Why Not	How Might You Resist?
...Natalie is kind of heartbroken and confused. I say this because she is looking at you with a blank expression on her face.	It is trying to get across the point that teenaged girls get confidence in knowing that someone they look up to has the same thing happen to her that happens to them.	Yes, because if you get dumped in middle school you can move on and it is not the end of the world.	...I don't think all success takes experence but I do think it is worth working for.
She is saying that many people get their hearts broken in their lives but it is not the end of the world.	If you take your chances with a relationship, your heart will be stomped on.	Yes, I agree with the message. Because everybody will get hurt, by a boy, girl or something.	Natalie Imbruglia seems pretentious & she has built an Image to sell records.
...all people are going to get hurt in there life, whether you are rich, famous, poor. Just keep going on with your life.	That even if you are hurt you can go on, and possibly become a stronger person for it all. Even pretty girls get dumped.	No. She is very stereotypical because she may have had a bad experience with men, that doesn't mean everyone will.	...tell my friends to not buy her CD's.
...a very opinionated feminist with a good voice.		The thing about pretty girls getting dumped is dumb. Who cares? Every one gets dumped.	
That she is strong but sensitive.			

Charles, who also resented the clerk's assumptions about children who attend private schools, pointed out, "I think that guy at the record store told you what we'd be listening to because we're a private school, and yet none of my friends would listen to that [Natalie Imbruglia's "Torn"]." When asked what he and his friends *would* consider worthwhile music, Charles said, "The Dave Matthews Band. Their songs are about real issues (teen pregnancy, sex, violence, and things). They're not overproduced by the media, and their videos go with the songs they sing." Several others nodded or voiced their agreement with Charles. But Amy was not so sure that the clerk had erred in his assumption. As she noted, "Your taste in music *does* depend on what's current with your peer group." And another girl, who had lived previously in a neighboring county that is comprised largely of farm families, attested to the fact that when she was part of that community she listened to a lot of country bluegrass music.

Before bringing the lesson to a close, I asked the students what they thought of my decision to mix popular culture texts with school-like tasks, such as asking them to answer a set of questions about the two CDs and then participate in a whole-class discussion. At first they looked puzzled, as if they were not sure what I had in mind by asking such a question. Dera stepped in and said, "You know, what do you think about bringing this stuff into class?" Judy's eyes lighted up. "I like it!" she said, and then added, "I think it's good that you're trying to understand us and our music. And you gave us something to listen to while we worked." Susan agreed, saying, "It's a good way to get our opinions. Normally kids talk more about stuff they're interested in."

At this point, Dera stepped in to ask another question. She wanted to know what the class would consider to be too much of a good thing, in terms of mixing popular culture texts with school-like tasks. One student stated, "If she [referring to me] had come dressed up as a Spice Girl." Not one to let an interesting opportunity pass by, Dera probed further. "Why," she asked, "would that turn you off?" The same girl responded, "Because adults are supposed to be mature, and you're always telling us why we shouldn't be irresponsible." Dera smiled and let the issue drop.

Reflecting on What Was Learned

As I look back on what was learned in doing a lesson that used popular culture texts to teach students about critical media literacy, I would have to say that all of us—the students, Dera, and myself—came away from the experience a bit smarter on several counts. I learned that this group of eighth graders was indeed capable of unpacking many of the messages delivered by the popular media. They were able to read and interpret the disparate elements of such messages in a way that signaled their understanding of how things that seem natural and commonsensical on the surface may be mined for deeper meanings. I also learned by grounding my lesson in a modified version of Cohen's (1998) strategy for teaching about the self and Other that I was able to detect a few students' understanding of what it means to be simultaneously both audience and performer. Although only a handful of the students demonstrated this understanding, I believe that with more time and similarly grounded lessons, I would be able to assist other students in developing the same level of understanding.

Although neither Dera nor I could say for sure how much of what the students said was said for our benefit, we felt fairly confident that we did not position them in such a way that they had little choice but to "disavow their 'secret pleasures'" (Luke, 1997, p. 43) in the two CDs that were presented as part of the lesson. Perhaps we avoided this common pitfall simply because the Spice Girls and Natalie Imbruglia were not held in very high regard by any of the students. Had we introduced Charles's favorite, the Dave Matthews Band, it is quite possible that we might have come close to stepping over the line that Luke and others (for example, Buckingham & Sefton-Green, 1994; Murdock, 1997) warn teachers against.

I also relearned the value of being up front and honest with adolescents. This particular group of eighth graders gave me the opportunity to try an idea with them that I had had little or no prior experience putting into practice. In return, they expected me to answer Alex's question about how I chose the Natalie Imbruglia CD. By being forthright in my response, I opened the discussion to a sensitive issue, at least in these eighth graders' eyes. However, they handled it well. My only regret is that I positioned the sales clerk, who was only doing his job by helping me identify an appropriate CD (at my request), in an unflattering light. In retrospect, I wish I had made that point clear when relating the story to the class.

Finally, in gathering materials in preparation for this lesson, I came to appreciate firsthand what James Brooks (1998), a high school teacher in Dayton, Ohio, had in mind when he wrote,

> Unless we intentionally close ourselves off from it, we are *all* bombarded these days with massive amounts of nonprint media. And what is true for adults is much more true for teenagers.... Popular culture is not just a teenage sidelight, it is the milieu in which they operate. David Denby, professional media critic, wrote in a recent article for *The New Yorker*, "for many [teenagers], pop has become not just a piece of reality—a mass of diversions, either good or bad, brilliant or cruddy—but the very ground of reality...." Pop culture is here to stay. (p. 21)

CHAPTER 6

Identities, Positioning, and Critical Media Literacy

With the remarkable development of faster and more accessible ways of communicating, trends and the "what's hot" for the moment seem to change even more quickly than before, and "updating" and "upgrading" have become part of our daily vocabulary. Staying current, in fact, is one of the most difficult tasks for teachers interested in incorporating popular culture texts in their instructional repertoire. For the sake of better serving students' needs, however, it has become necessary to take on this difficult task. Carmen Luke (1997) has argued "that if schooling refuses to deal with the texts of everyday life—which include media and school texts—then educators will indeed widen, not bridge, the experiential and knowledge gap between both teacher and student" (p. 47). Closing the classroom door on popular culture only causes it to go underground, according to Lewis (1998). It is better, then, that as educators we learn how to engage with students in examining some of the issues underlying media literacy in an age of popular culture.

We explore three issues in this chapter. First, we look to the literature for support in challenging a monolithic view of the media. Next, we explore how identities get constructed and positions get taken up or resisted. Finally, we relate identity construction and positionality to critical media literacy by using examples drawn from popular culture.

Challenging a Monolithic View of the Media

Buckingham and Sefton-Green (1994), who have done extensive research in popular culture studies, stated that there are vast differences in media consumer tastes. The fact that a popular culture text, such as a Madonna music video, is deemed part of mass media does not mean that all consumers read it the same way. In fact, according to Buckingham and Sefton-Green, popular culture texts become popular because they allow a range of readings, thus appealing to a wide audience. Although individuals of the same social group may have similar tastes in music, television programs, magazines, or any other popular commodity, their readings will differ. It would be presumptuous and even erroneous to think that an individual's reading of a particular media form is directly attributable to differences in gender, ethnicity, or some other identity factor (such as, class, religion, or age). Individuals vary within groups, and it is this variation that aids in the dispelling of a monolithic view of the media.

Identities and Positionings

The intimate link between one's language and identity is a well-known fact in the field of sociolinguistics. According to Le Page and Tabouret-Keller (cited in Tabouret-Keller, 1997, p. 315), "The language spoken by somebody and his or her identity as a speaker of this language are inseparable.... Language acts are acts of identity." This equating of one's language with one's identity is only part of the story, however. Context also matters. For example, Gee (1996) illustrates how language in the social context of a "biker bar" (pub) reveals much more about the narrator (Gee) than his proficiency in using English:

> Imagine I park my motorcycle, enter my neighborhood "biker bar," and say to my leather-jacketed and tattooed drinking buddy, as I sit down: "May I have a match for my cigarette, please?" What I have said is perfectly grammatical English, but is "wrong" nonetheless, unless I have used a heavily ironic tone of voice. It is not just *what* you say but *how* you say it. And in this bar, I haven't said it in the "right way." I should have said something like 'Gotta match?' or 'Give me a light, wouldya?'
>
> But now imagine I say the "right" thing ("Gotta match?" or "Give me a light, wouldya?"), but while saying it, I carefully wipe off the bar stool

with a napkin to avoid getting my newly pressed designer jeans dirty. In this case, I've still got it all wrong. In *this* bar they just don't do that sort of thing: I have *said* the right thing, but my "saying-doing" combination is nonetheless wrong. It's not just what you say or even how you say it, it's also who you are and what you're doing while you say it. It is not enough just to say the right "lines." (p. viii)

This excerpt is an example of Discourse, with a capital *D*. Briefly defined, Discourses, or what Gee (1996) has called "identity kits," are ways of speaking, seeing, thinking, and behaving that make it possible to recognize (and be recognized by) others like oneself. Whether in biker bars, such as the one just described, or in other social contexts, Discourses operate as ways of integrating and sorting individuals and groups.

Self and Group Identities

The examples that follow are useful in thinking about what distinguishes a person's self-identity from a group's identity. As Gee's (1996) example demonstrates, each of us has a perception of ourselves that may or may not be consistent with how others in various social groups view us. Discrepancies between self-identity and group identity can cause great concern and anxiety in young people, as Finders (1997) documented in her study of adolescent girls. In this study, group identity is privileged over individual identity to such an extent that some of the girls "boasted that teachers couldn't tell them apart if they were not together" (p. 49). For example, in an interview, one of the girls named Angie told Finders, "Ms. Jacobsen said that she didn't know me anymore cause I wasn't with Tiff" (p. 49). Angie and Tiffany were members of a group Finders named the Social Queens. They put much time, energy, and effort into looking and acting the same as everyone else in their group.* They also made it clear that boundaries existed between their particular social group and other

---

*According to Tabouret-Keller (1997): "Joining a group is in itself a very complex process involving factors linked with the subjects' most subjective and intimate history, their situation and status in society, etc. Hence identity is rather a network of identities, reflecting the many commitments, allegiances, loyalties, passions, and hatreds everyone tries to handle in ever-varying compromise strategies" (p. 321).

groups (for example, the Tough Cookies) by demonstrating their sense of allegiance and membership through fashions, attitudes, and media preferences. In fact, the Social Queens' sense of themselves was constructed largely through the media. For instance, they positioned themselves as "just regular teenagers" because the teen magazines they read (for example, *Sassy*, *YM*, *Seventeen*, and *Teen*) ritually supported this position.

Not all group identities are constituted as straightforwardly as the ones illustrated in Finders's (1997) work. An example of how popular culture is sometimes erroneously implicated in a group's identity construction can be seen in "gangsta" rap music. Although typically associated with black gang members who live in the "hood," gangsta rap finds some of its staunchest support coming from young white males. As the black feminist writer bell hooks (1994) has pointed out in her critique of this popular culture form, gangsta rap is not what it seems. Contrary to what we may have been led to believe, the violent and misogynist messages of gangsta rap are not perpetuated in a cultural vacuum in the "'hood'"; rather, these messages are "a reflection of the prevailing values in our society, values created and sustained by white supremacist capitalist patriarchy" (hooks, 1994, p. 26). Group identities are complex and are not always what they appear to be. Unless one understands how such identities get constructed, it is easy to position people in ways they might not position themselves.

Positioning

The two examples of positioning we include in this section are representative of the different power relations operating in any given context. In the first example, Lewis (1998) tells a story involving her son and how he was positioned by a teacher as being the stereotypical rebellious teenager.

> Recently, my thirteen-year-old son was stopped in the hallway by a teacher who questioned whether his T-shirt met the school's dress code. He wore a rock T-shirt depicting the dancing figures of women who would not be considered attractive according to media standards. Is the T-shirt meant to make a statement about the sexist images on most rock paraphernalia as my son explained it to me, or is it disrespectful as the teacher concluded? Had the teacher known that the rock band was an all-

female feminist band, would that change the teacher's interpretation of its message and her interactions with my son? (p. 116)

Later in the article, Lewis raises several important questions about what the teacher might have discovered had she taken the time to ask her son why he was wearing the T-shirt. Instead, by positioning him as someone who had not only broken the school's dress code, but also had trampled on the teacher's sensibilities, the teacher found it difficult to retract her original stance and understand the antisexist statement Lewis's son thought he was making.

The second example that follows demonstrates the distinguishing characteristics between interactive and reflexive positioning. According to Davies and Harré (1990), positioning is first and foremost a conversational phenomenon:

> [I]t is the discursive process whereby selves are located in conversations as observably and subjectively coherent participants in jointly produced story lines. There can be *interactive positioning* in which what one person says positions another. And there can be *reflexive positioning* in which one positions oneself. However, it would be a mistake to assume that, in either case, positioning is necessarily intentional. (p. 48)

As Davies and Harré go on to explain, the way speakers position one another and themselves directly shapes the very nature of the conversation. How such interactive and reflexive positionings play out in real life can be found in the following example:

> Rachel, an Asian American woman, is sitting with her colleague, Mona, a European American woman. They are discussing issues related to literacy education and school reform. Another European American woman who has never met Rachel walks into Mona's office. She and Mona speak briefly. After a bit, the woman turns to Rachel and asks, "So, how are students taught reading in your country?" Rachel and Mona look at each other, surprised. Mona finally breaks the silence by saying, "Rachel is an American." The woman blushes and says, "Oh," and remains relatively silent throughout the remainder of the meeting.

In this example, the woman who entered the room positioned Rachel as a foreigner. Rachel had several positions available to take up at this point. For example, she might have become irate and demanded an apology for such a racist comment; she might have laughed to herself and played along, as if she had just arrived in the country; or she might have remained speechless, unable to decide what position to take up.

Activity: Imagine yourself as one of the three people in the earlier example (Rachel, Mona, or the woman). Think about what position (any one of those offered or one of your own) you would take as that person. Tell whether the position you took up is an example of interactive or reflexive positioning. Do these different positionings enable you to better understand yourself or the other person? Why? Why not?

Identity Construction, Positionality, and Critical Media Literacy

One of the most visible ways in which the media positions young people is through popular culture texts that tend to create gendered identities. As discussed in Chapter 1, critical media literacy is concerned with enabling individuals to exert agency in deciding which of the many available positions they will take up or resist. According to Carmen Luke (1997), women have historically had little or no voice in how they were represented in the media:

> [W]omen's historical representations, whether in print or visual texts, have been primarily male-authored versions of girls, women, and "things feminine." The historical silencing of female authorship authority, in turn, has led to a fetishization and objectification of "the feminine" that, in various textual forms, reflects a collective male gaze and desire. Cultural industries in particular have a long history of male cultural productions of feminine stereotypes and misrepresentations that conceptualize women primarily either as objects of male adornment, pursuit, and domination, or as mindless domestic drudges, mentally vacant bimbos, or saintly supermoms. (p. 21)

The Barbie doll is a good example of what Luke (1997) meant by the media's powerful influence over young people's construction of gendered identities—girls, in developing their own such identities, and boys, in seeing girls as Barbie-like or "wanna-be" Barbies. Popular media celebrities, such as Pamela Anderson, formerly of the television show *Baywatch*, embody the traditional blonde bombshell image. From her Barbie-doll physique to her choice of an abusive ex-husband who is considered a "bad-boy" musician, Anderson symbolizes, to some people, contemporary popular culture's image of femininity and young womanhood. Yet another side of the popular Barbie icon is reflected in the lyrics from the song "Barbie Girl" by the Danish group Aqua.

The song "Barbie Girl" opens with Ken inviting Barbie to go for a ride. Barbie jumps into the car and sings about her life as a plastic doll. She invites the listeners to play out their fantasies with her. She declares herself the "blonde bimbo" and urges them to manipulate and create her vacuous super-feminine image.

Although the "Barbie Girl" song by Aqua is usually read as a sarcastic tribute to Barbie, it also contributes to young people's construction of gender. A note from Johan Otterud, the author of a Web site devoted to Barbie, states the following: "Chat with other Barbie

Figure 21
Barbie Girl Homepage

Barbie Girl Song Text—Johan Otterud's Homepage
http://hem1.passagen.se/otterud/barbiegirl/

Welcome to Johan Otterud's NEW! **Barbie Girl Homepage!**

Girl fans! And read some Aqua news (under construction). I will try to update the site as often as I can with new texts new links and new images! Enjoy!" The homepage of this Web site, which is shown in Figure 21, displays an image of Barbie that equates a seductive stare with femininity.

Steinberg (1997), a researcher interested in studying Barbie and young girls' readings of the Barbie image, has traced the origin of this popular culture icon:

> Where does the text of Barbie begin? Thirty-seven years ago, Mattel invested in the production of a slim, blonde doll who wore a variety of coordinated "outfits." While on vacation in Europe, Mattel's cofounder, Ruth Handler, discovered Lily. Lily was a prominent star of comics—a sexy blonde with loose morals who adorned the dashboards of men's autos throughout Germany and Switzerland. Her origin is not well documented, although her lineage has been traced to a Lily comic strip. Handler decided to bring the model of Lily with her back to the United States and create a doll that could wear multiple "outfits"—she would name her Barbie—after her daughter, Barbara. (p. 208)

Claims and recollections about the true origin of Barbie vary. As one of our reviewers noted, Barbie first emerged as a "rather hard looking (and scary) brunette in the late 1950s [who] evolved into a blue-eyed blonde with the emergence of California surfing music in the early 1960s." Whatever the origin of Barbie, her tradition of representing femininity has remained strong and steadfast through the decades.

The emphasis on multiple outfits, makeup, and fashion in the genesis of Barbie and the values such goods represent are replicated daily in the media. These highly prized commodities are featured in teen magazines, television advertisements, and the movies. What, if anything, can be done to counter such a normative view of what it means to be a girl? Because many young girls are socialized into these gendered identities long before they enter school, teachers may find it quite challenging to engage them in reflecting on how such Barbie-like images influence their thinking and acting. Girls are not the only consumers of the Barbie doll and Pamela Anderson popular culture texts; boys also read these texts and use them in constructing their own notions of masculinity.

Deconstructing the sexist messages and images of certain popular culture texts is difficult in its own right. As discussed previously in Chapters 1 and 2, Carmen Luke (1997) has cautioned against a pedagogy that forces students into confessing their secret pleasures and desires. At the same time, adult guidance is necessary if young people are to learn how the media's images of femininity and womanhood shape young girls' identities. Because sexist popular culture texts influence how boys and young men view their own masculinities, male students also need to learn how to deconstruct such texts. In the following section of this chapter, we illustrate how the media can both hinder and promote the deconstruction of negative gender stereotypes.

Walt Disney Movies, Fairy Tales, and Reconstructing Female Identities

The stereotypical images of Barbie also are replicated in Walt Disney movies and fairy tales. Walt Disney has been called "an icon of American culture [that] is consistently reinforced through the penetration of the Disney empire into every aspect of social life" (Giroux, 1997, p. 54). From movies to theme parks (such as, Disneyland, the "happiest place on earth"), the Walt Disney Corporation embodies U.S. consumerism and symbolism of innocence at its best. Disney has become the ultimate image-making industry. In fact, to criticize the romanticized notions of femininity in Disney movies is to step on many toes, in terms of what it means to be a child in the United States. With its "Teacher of the Year Awards" and scholarships to students, the Disney conglomerate aligns itself closely with educational values. Who can argue against such values? Yet we would wager that it is rare, indeed, for Disney movies and television shows to be accompanied by lessons involving critical media literacy.

Increasingly over the past several years, Disney productions have been criticized for their stereotypical, sexist, and patriarchal ideology. This ideology and its accompanying messages are present in movies such as *Sleeping Beauty*, *Pocahontas*, *Little Mermaid*, and *Cinderella*. In an effort to address such criticism and respond to demands for constructing a new feminine identity in modern times, Disney created the movie, *Mulan*, a story about a female Chinese teenager who wears a set of armor and fights in wars. In the June 18, 1998, issue of *USA Today*, writer Susan Wloszczyna proclaimed, "'Mulan' breaks the mold.... After 36 animated features in more than 60 years, Disney's cartoon heroines are finally free of the bonds of their Barbie doll figures and saccharine-spiked romances" (p. D1). However, Mulan does not go far enough to satisfy Kathleen Karlyn, an academic whose research area is girl culture. Karlyn (as cited in Bellafante, 1998) pointed out that Mulan still has to disguise herself as a boy to be a heroine. According to Karlyn, "We're beginning to think about heroism in a female way. But we don't have narratives or genres in which we can comfortably fit strong female protagonists" (p. 62).

Karlyn's point is central to the research Gilbert (1988) has been conducting for over a decade. Gilbert has argued that young girls' identities and the positions they take up indicate that they do not passively accept the media's representation of what it means to be a girl or woman; instead, they appear to be more critical than had been previously thought. Gilbert noted, "girls are more resistant to cultural images of romantic femininity than is sometimes assumed" (p. 13). For example, in the following story, "The Intelligent Princess," written by a 10-year-old girl (but retold and commented on by Gilbert), it is the princess, not the prince, who goes out on a quest. In doing so, she has several opportunities to resist romantic notions of what it means to be feminine and a princess.

> The intelligent princess has two encounters with men on her journey, and both are sexual. The prince of Mitredom runs out of his castle to meet her.
>
> "Will you marry me?" were the first words that came out of him. "I'll give you 800,000,000 bags of candy!"
>
> This "intelligent princess" naturally refuses such an offer:
>
> "Candy? Piffle. Candy? Pooh. An intelligent princess won't do for you!" she said boldly, and stomped off.
>
> However at her next stop—Greenwood Lake—she relaxes with her tuna sandwich, lemonade, bubble gum and pop music, only to hear a rustle in the bushes. A handsome prince has been spying on her. He invites her out that evening, but she rejects him, packs up and heads off again. "What a drag. I was having fun," she thought.
>
> The princess moves on to Green Glass castle, where she meets a third young man, a prince. This prince calls her "companion," and asks her her business. The conversation exchange between the two is noticeable for its apparent equality of power for the two speakers, and for the princess's forthrightness. The young prince decides to join the princess

on her quest (it is made clear in the narrative that it is the princess's quest), and at their first stop they meet a young child (also a prince), befriend him, and all go back to the princess's kingdom. A potential union between the prince and the princess is unspoken, but implied. But it is at the prince's suggestion: "I—ah—wouldn't mind coming home with you." (p. 17)

In this story, there are several incidents of resistance to the romantic notions of femininity. The story could be thought of as a rewriting of the fairy tales that are representative of so many Disney movies. However, the girl who narrated the story was still not able to break out of the marriage mold inherent in traditional fairy tales. Even though the princess was the one who went on a quest, the quest was to find a husband. The girl narrating the story did not take up all of the stereotypical princess images and messages from the fairy tale movies, but she also did not construct a self-empowering and liberated position that some feminist educators may have wanted to see in this reconstructed story. The story does show, however, ways for young girls to try on different identities and in doing so reconstruct their notions of femininity.

Pompe (1996) has suggested that participating in children's plays may encourage children to try on different gendered identities. By reconstructing their ideas of what it means to be male and female, children develop a certain flexibility that allows them to position themselves differently when reading popular culture texts. For example, to experiment with various positions that can be resisted or taken up, girls may play nurturing, submissive female roles in *Power Rangers* plays, or they may cast themselves as the assertive and dominant heroes in their originally composed *X-Men* plays (Dyson, 1997). This ability to try on various roles allows a more powerful reading of popular culture texts than, for example, children who consistently play it "safe" by assuming only positions of submission or domination all the time (Pompe, 1996).

Extending the Need for Reconstructing Gendered Identities to High School and Beyond

Just as with young children, there is a need to provide older students with opportunities to reflect on and reconstruct their notions of gender identities. This became obvious to Jennifer during a graduate course she took on women and minority representation in children's literature. During a class discussion about the lack of strong female identities in various versions of the Cinderella tales, some alarming comments were made by her classmates. Their remarks centered on the high school girls whom these graduate students taught and how the girls identified and positioned themselves. For example, one graduate student was gravely concerned about her female high school students who were aware that they could choose any career they wanted to pursue; but when it came to relationships with their male peers, they did not transfer their liberated ways of thinking about careers to their personal lives.

Similar kinds of messages about the positions young women take up were echoed in the undergraduate literacy methods class that Jennifer taught. The undergraduate students stated that they did not feel pressured by the media to dress and behave in particular ways; rather, it was pressure from their boyfriends, husbands, and male peers that caused them to make certain choices about their appearance.

Not only based on these discussions, but from related ones as well, it seemed to us that when issues of young women's identity formation are not addressed in the elementary, middle, and high school years they become part of adulthood and form a cycle, the effects of which are passed from one generation to the next. Thus, as Carmen Luke (1997) has advocated, it is incumbent on teacher education programs to incorporate critical media literacy studies as part of their curriculum.

As future classroom teachers, undergraduate students need opportunities to consider how the media influence their own lives before they can begin to appreciate the need to teach critical media literacy to their students. One way that teacher educators might provide such opportunities would be to keep an eye out for controversial issues related to popular culture texts. For example, a recent issue of *Time* featured a cover asking, "Is feminism dead?" with the television character Ally McBeal's face next to that of Gloria Steinem, Betty Friedan, and Susan B. Anthony. The writer of the story, Ginia Bellafante (1998), raised the following dilemma for feminism:

> [M]uch of feminism has delved into the silly. And it has powerful support for this: a popular culture insistent on offering images of grown

single women as frazzled, self-absorbed girls. Ally McBeal is the most popular female character on television. The show, for the few who may have missed it, focuses on a ditsy 28-year-old Ivy League Boston litigator who never seems in need of the body-concealing clothing that Northeastern weather often requires. Ally spends much of her time fantasizing about her ex-boyfriend, who is married and in the next office, and manages to work references to her mangled love life into nearly every summation she delivers. (p. 58)

Bellafante further noted that the present "flightiness" of feminism, after the serious feminist movement of the 1970s, has resulted in the coined term, "Duh Feminism" (p. 57).

As a class activity, undergraduate teacher education majors might be asked to respond to Bellafante's (1998) critique of Ally McBeal. For example, they might be asked if it is too simplistic and too broad a generalization to position contemporary women as being obsessed only with themselves and dangling on male affection. What should be made of the fact that the Ally McBeal show is created by David Kelley, a man? Is it fair to conclude that all young women in the 1990s act, behave, think, and feel like Ally McBeal? What alternative readings of Ally McBeal are possible? Choosing an activity of this sort to use with undergraduate classes can demonstrate the ephemeral nature of popular culture, for Ally McBeal is sure to be replaced by another popular culture icon in the near future.

Reflecting on What We Have Learned

As we have pointed out in this chapter, it is important to acknowledge the influence of the media in shaping young people's identities. However, the media's influence does not dictate what its consumers will necessarily take up or resist. Not all young people are collectively and mindlessly buying into the various popular culture texts available. What is important for us, as educators, to understand is *how* and *why* individual students decide to comply with or resist the stereotypical images in certain popular culture texts. When this is understood, we will have gone a long way toward validating the teaching of critical media literacy in grades K–12 and beyond.

CHAPTER 7

Where We Are and Where We Need to Go in Theory and Research

Leila Christenbury (1998), the editor of the *English Journal*, recently noted the following in her introduction to a themed issue on media literacy:

> There is a certain irony that...[as teachers we] are responsible for the fostering of our students' media literacy. The great majority of us in the profession today are at or near middle age, and that means that many of us did not grow up with music videos, VCRs, CDs, [or] the Internet.... Yet it is now part of our job in the late 1990s to not only "teach" media literacy but, in a special way, to understand its unique power and lure and to help our students discriminate, choose, manage, and assess that media. (p. 13)

We open this chapter with Christenbury's excerpt because we think it explains in large part why, compared to other areas of literacy research, relatively little has been done on media literacy, to say nothing of critical media literacy. For the most part, those who comprise the present-day community of literacy researchers grew up in an era quite different from the one currently experienced by children and adolescents. Today, according to Robert Donmoyer (1998), editor of *Educational Researcher*, "we live in a world of 'hard-copy minutes,' a world in which nuance and subtlety are less important than melodrama, and painstaking deliberation takes a back seat to 'spinning' and sloganeering" (p. 27). Knowing this makes it all the more important that researchers not underestimate the media's pervasive presence in our lives and particularly what can be learned from studying its influence on students in and out of school (Alvermann, Hinchman, Moore, Phelps, & Waff, 1998; Dyson, 1997; Luke & Roe, 1993).

Because we live in a world of "hard-copy minutes" (Donmoyer, 1998, p. 27), it is exceedingly important that our critical literacy skills are honed to perfection. Text-processing studies are no less important today than they were in the late 1960s, 1970s, and early 1980s (Ruddell, Ruddell, & Singer, 1994). In fact, the ways we filter media texts through our own prior knowledge and use various coding systems to communicate are reminiscent of the seminal work done by Smith (1971) and Goodman (1967).

Similarly, reader response theories—especially those labeled experiential theories of response (Beach, 1993)—are deeply implicated in the research on subjectivity, positioning, and audience highlighted here. For example, Rosenblatt's (1938, 1978) work has demonstrated the importance of focusing on socially contextualized events and on helping individuals discover the pleasures and satisfactions of texts. When the definition of text is expanded to include the kinds of experiences students have with a broad range of media texts, it is easy to see the relation of reader response theories to critical media literacy.

In this chapter, we synthesize and explore where the literacy field is and needs to go in terms of theory and research on critical media literacy. To do this, we examine in greater depth some of the issues raised in previous chapters, and in particular, the theory and research underlying those issues. First, we consider a few representative studies that have looked at literacy in relation to identity and desire. Next, we consider studies that have dealt with audience, and in particular how audiences are positioned by the media and with what consequences. Last, we draw from these studies some implications for future research and practice that we hope will situate critical media literacy as a topic of theoretical and practical importance squarely within the literacy community.

One final note—the body of literature that is examined here is limited to research involving students in the primary grades through secondary school. This seems a useful parameter given that we focused exclusively on those grade levels in Chapters 3 through 5 and drew heavily from our own experiences or from working with teachers at those grade levels in the remaining chapters. Thus, although there has been some excellent work done on using popular culture texts with adults (for example, Flood et al., 1994; Radway, 1984), that work will not be included here.

Literacy, Identity, and Desire

Imagining or transgressing life experiences is part of the pleasure associated with popular culture texts. Whether those texts take the form of printed texts, such as horror fiction and feminist avant-garde literature, or the form of objects (for example, *Power Rangers* figures), videos, movies, computer games, MTV, and the like, they are generally believed to be the media through which children, adolescents, and adults explore their identities and desires. Explanations for their appeal draw from a number of diverse theories. For example, psychoanalytic theories point to repression themes in horror fiction that bring readers of both print and images into contact with culturally forbidden practices. Readers can imagine themselves both the victims and victimizers in horror fictions generated to bring out themes of repression.

Horror Fiction and a Theory of Carnival

Another theoretical stance or lens through which to view horror fiction is Bakhtin's (1973) notion of *carnival*—a time in which authorized and controlled disorder is sanctioned so that cultural norms can be suspended temporarily in favor of creating spaces for hierarchies to be inverted and boundaries to be dissolved. Originating in Medieval times, carnival was a time for the lower classes to dress in costumes and generally have fun mocking the pretentiousness of the upper classes. More modern-day carnivals, such as the festival of Mardi Gras, have a similar atmosphere—one in which the rules are suspended temporarily for the enjoyment of all. According to Vinz (1996), who used Bakhtin's notion of carnival to frame her study of adolescents' penchant for horror fiction, this genre "satisfies their need to transgress accepted rules, proverbial wisdom, and conventional knowledge, albeit vicariously" (p. 15).

Vinz (1996) began her research by eliciting the responses of 600 twelve- to eighteen-year-olds, who were spread across five sites in the

United States, to a questionnaire about their reading preferences and habits. Of these 600 students, 346 indicated they read authors whom they defined as horror fiction writers (such as, V.C. Andrews, Stephen King, Christopher Pike, R.L. Stine, and Anne Rice). Of the 346 students, 221 read a horror novel monthly, 83 read several horror titles each month, and 42 read multiple horror titles weekly. Vinz followed up by interviewing 25 of the 42 students who reported reading multiple horror titles each week. Those who were interviewed represented a wide cross section of the United States and an equally diverse set of interests. For example, there were four racial groups represented, a variety of ethnicities, and three students who claimed tribal affiliations. They came from lower-middle- to upper-middle-class family backgrounds, and with the exception of one student who identified himself as a "loner," all others described themselves as participating in a well-rounded lifestyle (sports, music, studying, and socializing with friends who were not necessarily avid horror fiction readers).

From the 25 interviews, Vinz (1996) concluded the following, as she analyzed the students' responses to horror narratives:

> [Their reading] allows them to mock or transgress, as in Bakhtin's conception, an official world over which they have little control and less than enthusiastic regard. Three eighth-graders, echoing sentiments expressed by many of the adolescents, are particularly intrigued with the narratives' power to open spaces that challenge the world as it is" (p. 16).... By participating in horror/comic motifs that scoff at the official, these young readers are pleasured in ways that recall Bakhtin's conception of carnival laughter.... In *Rabelais and His World*, Bakhtin (1968) theorized that literature of the folk is a "renunciation of many deeply rooted demands of literary taste," celebrating the essence of carnival laughter to open "the potentiality of an entirely different world, of another order, another way of life" (pp. 3, 48). It is this potentiality to laugh at and celebrate other ways of being in the world that appeals to these adolescents. (pp. 17–18)

An Opportunity to Transgress Through "Wild Words"

In a second study that explored the relation of reading and writing to identity and desire, Harper (1996) introduced six 17-year-old girls, who were enrolled in her creative writing class in a multiracial-multiethnic high school in Ontario, Canada, to feminist avant-garde literature. Under Harper's direction as teacher-researcher, the young women met twice a week for 2½ months during class time as a study group. They read a total of 18 literary works by contemporary French, Anglo, Black, and Native Canadian writers, all of whom had been published in three of Canada's well-known journals for feminist avant-garde writing. All the works, in one way or another, transgressed conventional ways of writing (for example, rules of orthography, syntax, semantics) and blended different forms of writing (poetry and prose). Themes included mother-daughter and sister relationships, childhood friendships, violence, drug addiction, homelessness, and immigrant experiences. The study group was encouraged by Harper to "read and write wildness into their words—using feminist avant-garde literature as support" (p. 6) as they engaged in discussions, wrote in their journals, or composed creative pieces of their own in their spare time outside of class.

Harper (1996) used feminist psychoanalytic theory to interpret the results of her interviews with the young women as they spoke at length about their reactions to the literature. Applying psychoanalytic theory from a feminist perspective, as Harper used it, involved looking for instances of substitution and displacement—a process that took into account how the young women in her study went to great pains to distance themselves from a feminist identity by aligning themselves with women whom they perceived to be "the lucky ones" (a term they used to describe women who were not oppressed). This term simultaneously allowed them to disconnect their identities from the women in the avant-garde literature whom they perceived to be oppressed (the "unlucky ones"). They achieved this distancing in several ways, an example of which follows:

> Refusing a feminist identity, the young women made strong efforts to avoid naming or referencing gender, even when it seemed appropriate to do so. Rebecca, for example, in replying to a question about what she learned from the project, commented, "I like to know what other people in Canada are writing, and I like the idea of just experimenting with the form and knowing that there are other forms you can use. I learned things like that." Although the project was explicitly about "women" writers—a fact highlighted throughout the project—Rebecca resisted naming it as such, and instead used the nongendered term "people".... This occurred with other students, as well. For example, in response to a question about parental expectations, Zandra dismisses the

possibility gender might factor into different expectations for her brother with the comment, "It's an age thing." (Harper, 1996, p. 8)

In a similar manner, the young women in Harper's (1996) study resisted writing from a feminist perspective. Denise, for example, explained, "I'm glad they [feminist writers] can write like that, but I don't think I can.... I appreciate it, but...it isn't really my style. I kind of write—I don't know how I write—I just write" (Harper, 1996, p. 11). Other students also expressed their pleasure in writing from a personal style, as a form of escape, which according to Harper's psychoanalytic interpretation equates to a feminine style of writing that is both emotional and irrational. In her words, it is a style that

> maps neatly onto the problems of loss and connection that underlie female adolescent life, ...does not threaten femininity or heterosexual desire, ...[and] is certainly at odds with feminist avant-garde writing, which looks to the pleasures in writing publicly and politically subversively. (p. 11)

Why avant-garde feminist writing did not offer a more attractive option for young women writers perplexed Harper. She suspected one reason why they invested in a safer, more feminine and personalized style of writing was the desire to please, to be viewed as legitimate writers in a school curriculum that has long rewarded students who conform rather than subvert its practices. Another reason, she surmised, had to do with the desire for agency: "to see and produce themselves as unaffected by gender, race, or class oppression" (p. 9).

Power Rangers and Other Potent "Texts"

A third study that explored the relation of literacy to identity and desire involved a primary class in an area north of Cambridge, England. Pompe (1996) worked with a group of 6 eight- to ten-year-olds one morning a week for a term and a half. Over that time, the group moved from discussing their favorite videos to producing their own video magazine. Working from her belief that Disney, Mattel, and the youth division of Rupert Murdoch and Company have been able to deliver what children want better than any other social institution, including the school, Pompe set out to chronicle the children's popular culture experiences and to engage them in writing their own audio-visual texts.

Going into the study, Pompe described four convictions related to her belief that the entertainment industry was outstripping the school in its ability to influence children by providing them with the potent texts they desired. First, she was convinced that the pleasures children took in the media and popular culture ran deep and were not in fact vacuous, no matter how tasteless they might seem to her. Second, she was convinced that it was pointless to rely on a victimization schema to explain the entertainment industry's success; thus, she resisted the temptation to portray the industry as simply imposing its products on a helpless segment of the population. Rather, she saw the consumers (the students in her study) as having desires that wielded significant power in what was ultimately embraced or shunned. Third, Pompe was convinced that just as readers of printed texts are active meaning makers, so, too, are viewers and listeners of audio-visual texts. In her words, "Experienced viewers ride horror films like roller-coasters, shrieking but safe, because they know the narrative codes of the genre" (p. 99). Finally, Pompe was convinced that classrooms must become partnerships where children and teachers learn to nourish their own desires while simultaneously undertaking work that engages the other and respects the identities of each member in the partnership.

These four convictions reflect postmodernist theoretical positions, which Luke (1998) has shown to be supportive of critical media literacy. According to Luke, the postmodern turn has collapsed old boundaries between what used to be thought of as "high" and "low" culture, with the result being that everyday practices are now taken much more seriously and are deemed worthy of academic inquiry. The postmodern turn also has changed our way of viewing culture, from thinking of it as a fairly static concept to one that is constantly under renewal and reinvention as a result of global, corporate, and electronic media influences. These changes in turn have begun to affect how we view print literacy. Luke has pointed out the following:

> [A]s we move from an industrial to a post-industrial information economy, one in which print literacy is not obsolete but certainly substantially transformed, then surely we need broader definitions of knowledge, literacy and pedagogy which will include study of the intertextuality of imageries, texts, icons and artifacts of new information economies, of media and of popular culture. (p. 27)

Theoretically, then, Pompe's (1996) study of children's popular culture experiences and their effort to produce a video magazine fell within a postmodern theoretical frame. As such, it allowed her to interpret the children's actions and talk in a way that highlighted the multivocal and dynamical nature of the project. For example, Pompe was able to capture the children's multilayered response to media in a way that demonstrated the complexity involved in interpreting their utterances. She wrote the following:

> One moment the children were slavering over some juicy bit of gore they'd relished; the next they were denouncing with sanctimonious "internalized parent" voices the fact that small children shouldn't watch *Power Rangers* because it would lead them to go out and kill each other. Just like the illusion that the researcher can observe a situation without influencing it, the fact that children say and mean different things in different situations and in front of different people cautions against a simplistic interpretation of their utterances. (p. 103)

Pompe was also able to demonstrate the futility of expecting children to take certain critical literacy strategies and run with them. Time and again she had to step in as the responsible adult and educator. For instance, when the children demonstrated they were "almost completely powerless when it came to harnessing their own skills and taking charge" (p. 101), Pompe intervened to bring the next stage of the project to fruition. This kind of intervention is exactly what Luke (1998) has argued for in her denunciation of pedagogical practices that valorize an "anything goes" type of response to the media and popular culture. In sum, what Pompe showed was the importance of disengaging from any notion of the teacher being able to simply hand over the tools of critique to children. The teacher's authority and power are not to be played down in a postmodern approach to critical media literacy.

Media Audiences

Mass media often is referred to as an amorphous lump that includes "television, radio, videos, newspapers, alternative 'zines, Hollywood cinema, billboards, web sites, video games" and so on, according to Lumby (1997). She opposes this conception of the media for the very reason that it implies a homogeneous and passive audience. In Lumby's words:

> The "mass" in media refers to audience reach rather than inherent homogeneity.... The idea that the media is a monolithic institution which somehow speaks in the voice of mainstream patriarchy (with a capitalist accent) is ultimately unhelpful.... To use an old postmodern metaphor, the media is like a virus. It infects everything it touches, but it is also, in turn, changed by what it comes into contact with—it mutates. (p. xxiii)

This definition of the media argues for the view that the meaning of a written message, a visual image, or a sound bite rests not in the thing itself but instead in us, the audience—the reader, the viewer, the listener. We are the ones who make meaning through a complex and mediated relationship with things (real or imagined objects, people, events, ideas), the concepts we hold of these things, and the language we use to communicate such concepts.

Just as the media is no monolithic institution, neither is an individual's self a monolithic entity—a point made Valerie Walkerdine (1990) in *Schoolgirl Fictions*, when she reminded us of the multiple subjectivities we each take up, or resist, as a consequence of the different positions available to us in any given context. Thus, as members of a media audience, every statement we make about texts that we read, hear, or view also raises "a bristling array of silences—things we could have said instead, aspects of a topic we could have highlighted but chose not to" (Freebody, Luke, Gee, & Street, in press, p. 1). Reasons behind the choices that we make when speaking out or remaining silent are inherently tied to how we perceive ourselves in relation to others, to what we are willing to reveal about our own interests and desires, and to whether or not we believe we can make a difference by adding our voices to the mix.

The complexities surrounding media audiences and how such audiences are positioned have emerged as key points of discussion in several critical literacy studies. Two of these studies are described next. The first was a study of how adolescents positioned themselves and others during after-school talk about a variety of popular culture texts in a public-library setting in a town in northeastern Georgia (Alvermann, Young, & Green, in press). The second study (Robinson, 1997) examined the ways in which children in a British primary school in England's southeastern sector used their television viewing experiences to interpret the appropriateness of certain print narratives.

After-School Talk About Popular Culture Texts

In framing their study of adolescents' after-school talk about a variety of popular culture texts, Alvermann et al. (in press) drew from a theoretical framework that views literacy and discourse as critical social practices and locates such practices in the interplay within and across three contexts: the situation-specific or local context, the institutional context, and the societal context (Fairclough, 1989, 1995). This broad array of contexts offered the researchers multiple opportunities to observe the dynamics involved as the 20 adolescents, grouped into four Read and Talk (R&T) Clubs, took turns positioning one another as audience and performer in ways that moved the analysis in interesting directions. Framing the study so that it took into account the interplay within and across the three contexts (local, institutional, and societal) made it possible to use critical discourse analysis (Fairclough, 1989, 1995) as a method for teasing out certain political issues, such as those related to power and ideology.

Twenty adolescents (middle and high school students from a variety of area schools) and two adults met weekly for 15 weeks in a small library as members of four after-school Read and Talk Clubs. Primary data sources included the adolescents' daily activity logs, the researchers' field notes, transcripts of taped R&T Club discussions, and transcripts of interviews with the adolescents and their parents. As club members, the adolescents negotiated among themselves concerning the types of materials (for example, popular fiction, teen magazines, sports magazines, newsletters about UFO sightings) they would read and discuss at their weekly meetings. It was during these negotiations and when they constructed themselves as audience in their respective R&T Clubs that members engaged in positioning one another. Although they were particularly adept at fashioning new subjectivities as they engaged with different forms of popular culture and brought outside media influences into their discussions, by far the more interesting positioning to observe occurred as the adolescents interacted with one another in their R&T Clubs.

For example, one group had fun trying on their new personas as they discussed elements of their favorite magazines. Noting a reticence on the part of the girls in the group to talk beyond a superficial level about the contents of a particular teen magazine, Colin (the adult facilitator) inquired why this was so. Rhiannon said that she would never discuss something in the group that had been written specifically for girls for fear of what the boys would say. Then, turning to address the two boys, Tommy and Jason, she asserted confidently, "I wouldn't talk about something [girl talk] you boys wouldn't understand." Pressed as to why she felt they would not understand, Rhiannon simply added, "It's a given!" (Alvermann et al., in press). Similar patterns of interaction occurred during discussions of Rhiannon's and Rose's favorite books in the popular Sweet Valley High series, which is known for its stereotyping of adolescent females. In Rhiannon's words, the series is written "from a girl's point of view" (Alvermann et al., in press) When books in this series were the topic of discussion, Colin wrote in his field notes that questions or comments from the audience by Tommy, Jason, or himself received scant, if any, consideration from the four female participants.

Rhiannon's reference to "girl talk" as something that males in the audience would not understand is a form of female discursive resistance. According to Brodkey (1989), this type of resistance calls for "re-presenting a stereotype as an agent in a discourse [which is] the least committed to preservation of that stereotype—as Toni Morrison does when representing Afro-American women as the agents rather than the victims of events in her novels" (p. 127). In a similar manner, Rhiannon used girl talk (a negative cultural stereotype) to her advantage by demonstrating that a mere mention of the fact males would not understand her favorite teen magazine or the Sweet Valley High books could effectively preclude the male point of view from being considered.

Giving agency to girl talk as a form of communication that males reputedly demean (and thus would not understand) is one way of resisting old discourses and opening new and contradictory ways of thinking about the male-female binary. At the same time, the very act of engaging in essentialist talk, as in Rhiannon's case, served to inscribe still further the stereotypes surrounding male and female preferences in reading materials in larger societal contexts. On only one occasion did we see such essentializing talk challenged. That occasion involved yet another discussion in Colin's Wednesday R&T Club, one

131

in which Rhiannon had commented to the group that "boys spend all their time talking about sports," partly in reference to Tommy's obsession with sport magazines. Jane, referring to the fact that she read swimming magazines, strongly disagreed, saying, "me and my friends talk about sports, we're competitive, and we're all girls" (Alvermann et al., in press).

Like the adolescents' essentializing talk in the Wednesday R&T Club, television programming is also said to have techniques for gendering its audience (Buckingham, 1993a; Fiske, 1987). In the study that follows, however, Robinson (1997) found that children's variation in engaging with television or print narratives seemed generally to depend more on their motivation and interest in the task than on any difference attributable to gender. However, there were some interesting exceptions to this pattern, and it is to these that we now turn.

Television Viewing, Book Sorting, and Gender Awareness

The centrality of narrative texts in human experience, generally, and in both television and print literacy, specifically, prompted Robinson (1997) to argue for narrative as the primary theoretical site where language, thought, and culture intersect. Drawing from Vygotsky's (1934/1962) work and from media studies and literary theory to frame her school-based case study, Robinson set out to discover how a small group of 8- and 9-year-olds would respond to a series of tasks involving television and print narratives. What she learned was that the children basically used the same strategies to "read" the two kinds of narratives. But what is of interest here is the audience portion of her research.

Tasks specific to determining audience appropriateness and appeal were piloted prior to the start of Robinson's main field work. As part of those pilot tasks, children grouped both television programs and books by their perceptions of the intended audience (gender and age) and by their predictions of how the audience would react. For the main study, titles of television programs were drawn from those that occurred most frequently in the children's viewing diaries. A book-sorting exercise also was used in the main study. Both mixed- and single-sex groupings were used. Working in small groups of three or four, "the children were asked to complete a grid to show which television programmes and books they felt were appropriate for younger children, inappropriate for younger children but appropriate for themselves, and inappropriate for anyone except adults" (Robinson, 1997, p. 82). Children also were asked to imagine that members of the opposite-sex group were coming to their house and to suggest appropriate viewing titles for them.

Findings revealed that the children were highly aware of gender appropriateness or inappropriateness for both television and book narratives. According to Robinson (1997), this "led to a tension between girls and boys and a solidarity of approach from the girls" (p. 75). Each sex succeeded in provoking the other by positioning its members in uncomplimentary ways (for example, the boys tagged certain titles "girly, girly" or "soppy") and by overgeneralizing (for example, the girls claimed the boys would watch nothing but football). Like Buckingham (1993a) found, however, there was much more ambivalence on an individual basis. For example Robinson noted the following:

> In a task...which involved sorting a pile of books into self-chosen categories, the girls had been keen to use the groupings "Girls' Books" and "Boys' Books" but had been unable to proceed. Although they were convinced of the existence in general terms of these categories, every time they tried to place a book, one of the group would object. If it was being suggested as a boys' book, one of the girls had always enjoyed it; if as a girls' book, then someone had disliked it. (p. 72)

Gender awareness was also an issue in terms of mothers and daughters colluding when it came to television viewing in male-dominated families. Much like Sarland's (1991) findings from work done with adolescent audiences, Robinson (1997) discovered that primary-age girls and their mothers were adept at subverting the fathers' control over television viewing. In the example that follows, Natalie and Alexis reveal how this occurred:

Natalie: *Home and Away, Neighbours, Freddy's Revenge,* Mummy doesn't like that very much but...

Robinson: But they'd choose that for you to watch.

Natalie: Yeah.

Alexis: My dad's really fussy, he never lets me watch horror films or rude films.

Natalie: No, nor does my dad.

Robinson: So what would he choose?

Alexis: *Strike it Lucky*, *Wogan*, comedy shows, but my mum lets me watch all the horrors and rude films. (p. 66)

Alexis also told of her mother waiting for the father to fall asleep or leave the house before allowing her to change channels. But subverting the male's authority in the household seemed to work for girls only when their mothers colluded in the effort. For example, Robinson (1997) reported several instances in which the girls complained of having to give in to their brothers' viewing preferences. In the sibling audience, at least, brothers' preferences took precedence over sisters' and often led to the girls retreating to their rooms.

In sum, based on the two studies just described, middle school and high school students, as well as primary-level students, seemed astutely aware of gender differences when it comes to being positioned (or positioning others). Whether they perceived those differences while playing audience to their peers or while engaging in some fairly explicit attempts to mediate an unpleasant situation, the students demonstrated they knew how "doing gender" (West & Zimmerman, 1987) works in the media world.

Implications for Research, Theory, and Practice

Issues that involve children's identities, their desires, and how they find themselves positioned (and positioning others) in their role as audience to a variety of media texts have surfaced repeatedly in the chapters preceding this one. In fact, as a result of their prevalence, these issues became the foci of our more in-depth look at some of the relevant theories and research projects that have attempted to address identity, desire, audience, and positioning in the past. In the concluding part of this chapter, we look again to these issues—only this time, we consider the implications they hold for research/theory and practice. To avoid implying that we take a dichotomous view of research and practice (or theory and practice), we prefer to think of them more broadly as *praxis*, in the sense of "practice in action" (Sholle & Denski, 1993, p. 301). For us, praxis connotes a relation between research/theory and practice in that each informs and is informed by the other.

Usefulness of Critical Theory as a Framework for Research

When we decided to use the word "critical" to modify media literacy in the title of this book, we did so with the concept of critical theory in mind. This decision subsequently influenced the types of research we reviewed and the activities we included in the various chapters. If critical theory is a new concept for you, or even if you know a great deal about it and its premises, we believe you will find Hinchey's (1998) retelling of a Zen parable (see the following excerpt) and her analysis of that parable quite helpful. We also believe that reading her analysis of the parable will explain in part why we are partial to critical theory and find it useful as a framework for research on teaching critical media literacy in an age of popular culture.

> In a Zen parable, a young fish asks an elder fish to define the nature of the sea. The young one complains that although everyone talks constantly about the sea, he can't see it and he can't really get a clear understanding of what it is. The wise elder notes that the sea is all around the young one; it is where he was born and where he will die; it is a sort of envelope, and he can't see it because he is part of it.
>
> Such is the difficulty of coming to understand our own cultural beliefs and how they influence our actions. Like the fish who has trouble understanding the very sea surrounding him, we have trouble identifying the influence of our culture because we are immersed in it and are part of it; we have been since birth and we will be until death—or until an experience with a different culture shows us that things might be other than the way we've always known them to be.
>
> It is in overcoming this difficulty that critical theory is especially valuable. It offers us a new perspective to use in analyzing our experiences, as the fish would get an entirely new perspective on the sea if he were able to consider it from a beach. The lens of critical theory refocuses our vision of the place we've lived all our lives. As is true of all theory, the usefulness of critical theory is that it helps open our minds to possibilities we once found unimaginable. (Maybe standardized tests aren't reliable. Maybe tracking promotes inequality rather than equality.) Once such heresies are imagined, we can explore them. And maybe in our explorations, we can change the face of the way things *are*, forever. (Hinchey, 1998, p. 15)

Researchers who are interested in studying popular culture often frame their projects within a critical perspective because they are looking for ways of unpacking certain assumptions about this phenomenon that most of us take for granted—for just the way things *are*. The well-known author Toni Morrison (writing in *The Bluest Eye*, 1970) is reported to have observed the following about one such unquestioned assumption that deals with popular culture:

> Adults, older girls, shops, magazines, newspapers, window signs—all the world had agreed that a blue-eyed, pink-skinned doll was what every girl treasured. "Here," they said, "this is beautiful, and if you are on this day 'worthy' you may have it." (Morrison cited in Hinchey, 1998, p. 17)

In terms of critical theory, this remark attributed to Morrison demonstrates how the values of one group, with the help of the media, were judged to be the standard or "norm" against which all other dolls were evaluated. The fact that there might be little girls in the world for whom blue eyes and pink skin are not considered "beautiful" (or at least not the only combination of eye and skin color possible) is overlooked, consciously or unconsciously, as the case may be. Either way, when people construct their conceptions of other people, places, and things as "natural" or just the way things *are*, critical theorists would say that the more powerful group is trying to achieve hegemony over the less powerful group. As Hinchey (1998) has noted, "When hegemony is operating, the less powerful do as they're told and accept the inferior roles assigned to them without question" (pp. 19–20). It is this sort of disequilibrium that leads some researchers to consider the benefits of a critical framework for unpacking certain assumptions underlying hegemonic practices.

Some Objections to Using Critical Theory

All theories have both benefits and disadvantages attached to them, and such is the case for critical theory. One common objection to critical theory as a framework for research is that it is political. Those who raise this objection point to the fact that research that openly challenges the status quo is ideologically driven. Although this critique is valid, researchers who subscribe to critical theory are quick to point out that an unstated and unexamined assumption is that other theories driving literacy research are "neutral" or at least benign. Choosing between theories, themselves, is a political act. In even the most stringent of experimental designs—in which every variable is controlled to the greatest extent possible—the researcher will make decisions about which tests to apply or which measures to use that are influenced by the theory (or theories) he or she holds dear.

A second objection to critical theory is that it engenders despair. Researchers point out that the unequal distribution of wealth, privilege, and power are merely adding to the problems and dissatisfaction of those who are less privileged and powerful. This argument fuels hegemony in that less powerful groups unquestioningly accept their lot, thereby supporting the more powerful groups' contention that this is just the way things are. As Hinchey (1998) has explained the situation:

> This is more hegemony at work, more unquestioning acceptance that the way things are is the way they must be. But, in reality, there is only one certainty in current conditions: things are unlikely to change significantly if the less privileged and powerful are kept blind to the kinds of lives others live. If they can't imagine the kind of privilege others enjoy, then they can't *pursue* similar privileges—a larger piece of the pie—for themselves. And *that* is an obvious advantage for those who currently have power. (p. 145)

Finally, a third objection, and one that contradicts the previous one, is that critical theory is too idealistic. The assumption behind this charge is that to live and compete in a late capitalistic society one must look out for oneself. Notions of social justice are thought to be too utopian and unreachable. However, researchers who use critical theory to frame their work argue that while it may be idealistic to think it is possible to change the world, doing nothing is not an acceptable alternative. They shun cynicism in the belief that having a vision for how the world might be made a more just place is a goal worth working toward (Hinchey, 1998). The "utopia" they seek is a not an imaginary one "but in [the] sense of a future society of transformed social relations realizable through political action" (Sholle & Denski, 1993, p. 318).

Research Directions for Improving Practice

Among the studies that have looked at media literacy from a critical perspective, most have focused on younger children (e.g.,

Buckingham, 1993a; Cherland & Edelsky, 1993; Dyson, 1997; Gilbert & Taylor, 1991; Grace & Tobin, 1998; Hodge & Tripp, 1986; Lewis, 1997; MacGillivray & Martinez, 1998). Of those that have focused on adolescents (Buckingham & Sefton-Green, 1994; Finders, 1996; Fiske, 1989a, 1989b; Harper, 1996; Neilsen, 1998; O'Brien, 1998; Vinz, 1996), a common finding is that teens, while *not* as easily deceived by the mass media as some critics would assert, still find their personal needs for dealing with popular culture texts largely ignored and unaccommodated in formal education circles. This condition, we would argue, stems not so much from intentional neglect as from an older generation's lack of experience in dealing with the genre. Increasingly, researchers are becoming aware of gender's unstable role in media consumption practices. This is so, Ang (1996) has argued, because "gender identity...is both multiple and partial, ambiguous and incoherent, permanently in process of being articulated, disarticulated, and rearticulated" (p. 125). In short, stereotypical views of gender cannot fully account for the tastes of media audiences.

Although reading is one of the primary means for constructing gendered identities and negotiating their meaning in Western cultures, the nature of reading practices as they intersect with gender is one of the least-studied aspects of literacy education (A. Luke, 1994). When such practices have been researched, the issues that usually garner attention are gender equity and stereotyping. Although these are important issues, they do not shed light on what Sholle and Denski (1993) refer to as "the *affective investments* that students bring to a text" (p. 312). For example, if students know and can see that a particular magazine, video game, or television program is sexist in the way it represents males and females, do they still invest time in it and why? What meaning do they attach to their investment? These are research questions that need asking—not for the purpose of condemning young people's choices—but for expanding what we know about gender and how it intersects with media literacy. They are also questions, which if answered, could provide a better understanding of "meaning as *a contested event*, a terrain of struggle in which individuals take up often conflicting subject positions in relation to signifying practices" (McLaren & Lankshear, 1993, p. 385).

Misconceptions About the Practice of Critical Media Literacy

Common misconceptions persist about what teaching critical media literacy using popular culture texts should entail. One such misconception has to do with the belief that critical media literacy should help students learn how to liberate themselves from texts that are designed to dupe them. One way a teacher may fall prey to this pedagogical trap is to ask students to critique the media texts that they find pleasurable. As Carmen Luke (1994) had noted, asking students to do this "is likely to cue a critical response which can often be an outright lie...[for while] students are quick to talk a good anti-sexist, anti-racist, pro-equity game,...what [they] write in the essay or what they tell us in classroom discussion is no measure of what goes on in their heads" (p. 43). To avoid putting students in positions in which they can only recognize pleasure as a form of deception, Carmen Luke (1994) has argued for self-reflexive critical practice on teachers' parts:

> Although self-reflexivity has become somewhat of a cliché in educational circles, I am convinced that self-reflexive critique of our own pedagogies and political assumptions as media educators is paramount if we wish to avoid mechanistic transmission model pedagogies in which students are made to reproduce the teacher's preferred ideological take on the subject matter.... Media educators need to be mindful of the politics inherent in their textual selections and the critical textual practices they advocate because some choices can easily condemn youth's cultural terrain. (p. 43)

Similarly, Buckingham (1993c) has cautioned teachers about the dangers of critiquing children's pleasures in popular media. He has suggested that teachers take time to engage with different media for which they have no background experience (such as, computer games) in order to get a sense of what their students find so enjoyable. Doing so does not equate to some naive celebration of popular culture, nor does it necessarily lead to an appropriation of students' outside interests in the service of schooling. Rather, it serves as an introduction to what students value and find motivational.

Another misconception of what is involved in teaching critical media literacy using popular culture texts resides in the notion that "critical thinking" refers simply to the cognitive processing of ideas that literacy educators have traditionally associated with critical reading. As McClaren (cited in Sholle & Denski, 1993) has pointed out, "In their discussion of 'critical thinking' the new conservatives and liberals have neutralized the term *critical* by repeated and imprecise usage, removing its political and cultural dimensions and laundering its analytic potency to mean 'thinking skills' " (p. 319). A critical approach to media literacy focuses on the production and consumption of popular culture texts in the context of their own historical, political, and economic existence.

The Teacher's Role

What *is* our role as educators—do we interrogate, accept, support, or ignore our students' stances and preferences in terms of the popular media? We think there are at least two answers to that question, both of which deal with issues of identity and authority.

An effective pedagogical intervention, according to Sholle and Denski (1993), "must allow students to speak from their own experiences at the same time that it encourages them to identify and unravel the codes of popular culture that may work to...silence and disempower them" (pp. 307–308). This call for students to assume some authority on their own behalf when engaging with the popular media is grounded in the belief that to be media literate they must be aware of the multiple ways in which texts position them. It also requires that students be able to identify texts that express contradictory messages (in terms of ideological perspectives) and how taking up or resisting such messages can open spaces for imagining other possible worlds. Reading popular culture texts is never an innocent act. Identity and desire are inherently bound in the politics of such texts, a fact that becomes particularly relevant when such texts are being considered for classroom use. For as Worthy (1998) has shown so clearly in her study of two sixth-grade boys, Jared and Chase—youngsters she refers to as "renegade readers" (p. 509)—limiting the choice of what is read in schools can squelch children's interests in reading. Such squelching, if repeated over a period of years, can vastly alter how students see themselves as readers.

Effective interventions that use critical media literacy as a focus must avoid reproducing what Luke (1998) calls "the tyranny of authoritarian transmission models...[while simultaneously avoiding] slipping into a vacuous celebration of difference and rampant pluralism" (p. 35). To maintain an appropriate balance between the two extremes, it is important that teachers not abdicate their positions of authority. The risks involved in giving up such authority have been demonstrated in several studies. For example, the students in both Alvermann's (1996) and Ellsworth's (1989) classrooms experienced the disempowering effects of an absence of pedagogical authority during discussions in which they were encouraged to speak openly of their differences while their teachers attempted to maintain a so-called neutral or impartial stance. Attempts such as these must be examined in light of what Fairclough (1989) has described as *hidden power*— the act of disguising and downplaying one's authority in order to keep it. Put more bluntly, in Luke's (1998) terms, "pedagogy without a locus of authority...risks deceit" (p. 31).

Summary

Teaching critical media literacy using popular culture texts is currently an undertheorized and underresearched topic in the field of literacy education. Yet its relevance for teaching and learning in the 21st century has never been greater. As the media continue to find ways of producing texts for imagining or transgressing life experiences, it will become increasingly important to engage students in reading critically for the assumptions underlying those texts. The complexities surrounding media audiences, including issues of identity, desire, and positionality, suggest a range of research possibilities. Although in this book we have advocated a critical theory perspective for exploring such possibilities, any of a number of other theoretical frameworks are also viable. What is most important, we believe, is a concerted effort by practitioners and researchers alike to understand how reading, writing, listening, speaking, thinking, and viewing are attendant processes in the larger social, cultural, and political milieu that make up critical media literacy.

References

Alvermann, D.E. (1996). Introducing feminist perspectives in a content literacy course: Struggles and self-contradictions. In D.J. Leu, C.K. Kinzer, & K.A. Hinchman (Eds.), *Literacies for the 21st century: Research and practice* (Forty-fifth Yearbook of the National Reading Conference, pp. 124–133). Chicago, IL: National Reading Conference.

Alvermann, D.E., Hinchman, K.A., Moore, D.W., Phelps, S.F., & Waff, D.R. (Eds.). (1998). *Reconceptualizing the literacies in adolescents' lives*. Mahwah, NJ: Erlbaum.

Alvermann, D.E., Young, J.P., & Green, C. (in press). Adolescents' perceptions and negotiations of literacy practices in after-school Read and Talk Clubs. *American Educational Research Journal*.

Ang, I. (1996). *Living room wars: Rethinking media audiences for a postmodern world*. London: Routledge.

Baker, C.D., & Luke, A. (Eds.). (1991). *Towards a critical sociology of reading pedagogy*. Amsterdam and Philadelphia, PA: John Benjamins.

Bakhtin, M.M. (1968). *Rabelais and his world* (H. Iswolsky, Trans.). Cambridge, MA: Massachusetts Institute of Technology Press.

Bakhtin, M.M. (1973). *Problems of Dostoyevsky's poetics* (R.W. Rotel, Trans.). Ann Arbor, MI: Ardis.

Bakhtin, M.M. (1981). *The dialogic imagination*. Austin, TX: University of Texas Press.

Barthes, R. (1975). *The pleasure of the text*. New York: Hill and Wang.

Beach, R. (1993). *A teacher's introduction to reader-response theories*. Urbana, IL: National Council of Teachers of English.

Bean, T.W., Bean, S.K., & Bean, K.F. (1998, May). *Are adolescents reading more today, or less?* Paper presented at the 43rd Annual Convention of the International Reading Association, Orlando, FL.

Bellafante, G. (1998, June 29). Feminism: It's all about me! *Time*, 54–62.

Blak. (1998, June). [Letter to the editor]. *The Source*, p. 24.

Britzman, D. (1991). Decentering discourses in teacher education: Or, the unleashing of unpopular things. *Journal of Education, 173*(3), 60–80.

Brodkey, L. (1989). On the subjects of class and gender in "The literacy letter." *College English, 54,* 125–141.

Brooks, J. (1998). Teenagers evaluating modern media. *English Journal, 87*(1), 21–24.

Bruce, B.C. (1997). Literacy technologies: What stance should we take? *Journal of Literacy Research, 29,* 289–309.

Buckingham, D. (1993a). *Children talking television: The making of television literacy.* London: Falmer.

Buckingham, D. (1993b). Going critical: The limits of media literacy. *Australian Journal of Education, 37*(2), 142–152.

Buckingham, D. (1993c). Just playing games. *The English & Media Magazine, 28,* 21–25.

Buckingham, D. (Ed.). (1998). *Teaching popular culture: Beyond radical pedagogy.* London: University College London Press.

Buckingham, D., & Sefton-Green, J. (1994). *Cultural studies goes to school: Reading and teaching popular media.* London: Taylor & Francis.

Cherland, M.R., & Edelsky, C. (1993). Girls and reading: The desire for agency and the horror of helplessness in fictional encounters. In L. Christian-Smith (Ed.), *Texts of desire: Essays on fiction, femininity, and schooling* (pp. 28–44). London: Falmer.

Christenbury, L. (1998). From the editor. *English Journal, 87*(1), 13.

Christian-Smith, L. (1997). Pleasure and danger: Children, media and cultural systems. In S. Muspratt, A. Luke, & P. Freebody (Eds.), *Constructing critical literacies* (pp. 51–58). Cresskill, NJ: Hampton Press.

Cintron, R. (1991). Reading and writing graffiti: A reading. *The Quarterly Newsletter of the Laboratory of Comparative Human Cognition, 13,* 21–24.

Cohen, P. (1998). On teaching arts and "race" in the classroom. In D. Buckingham (Ed.), *Teaching popular culture: Beyond radical pedagogy* (pp. 153–176). London: University College London Press.

Davies, B., & Harré, R. (1990). Positioning: The discursive production of selves. *Journal for the Theory of Social Behavior, 20*(1), 43–63.

Deleuze, G., & Guattari, F. (1987). *A thousand plateaus.* Minneapolis, MN: University of Minnesota Press.

Donmoyer, R. (1998). This issue: Talking power to "truth." *Educational Researcher, 27*(1), 4, 27.

Dyson, A.H. (1997). *Writing superheroes: Contemporary childhood, popular culture, and classroom literacy.* New York: Teachers College Press.

Ellsworth, E. (1989). "Why doesn't this feel empowering?" Working through the repressive myths of critical pedagogy. *Harvard Educational Review, 59,* 297–324.

Fairclough, N. (1989). *Language and power.* London: Longman.

Fairclough, N. (1995). *Critical discourse analysis: The critical study of language*. London: Longman.

Finders, M.J. (1996). Queens and teen 'zines: Early adolescent females reading their way toward adulthood. *Anthropology and Education Quarterly, 27*(1), 71–89.

Finders, M.J. (1997). *Just girls: Hidden literacies and life in junior high*. New York: Teachers College Press.

Fiske, J. (1987). *Television culture*. London: Methuen.

Fiske, J. (1989a). *Reading the popular*. London: Unwin Hyman. (reprinted by Routledge, 1995)

Fiske, J. (1989b). *Understanding popular culture*. London: Routledge.

Fiske, J. (1994). Audiencing: Cultural practice and cultural studies. *Handbook of Qualitative Research*. Thousand Oaks, CA: Sage.

Flood, J., Lapp, D., Alvarez, A., Romero, A., Ranck-Buhr, W., Moore, J., Jones, M.A., Kabildis, C., & Lungren, L. (1994). *Teacher book clubs: A study of teachers' and student teachers' participation in contemporary multicultural fiction literature discussion groups* (Reading Research Rep. No. 22). Athens, GA: National Reading Research Center, Universities of Georgia and Maryland.

France, K. (1998, June). The "torn" bird. *Spin*, 76–80.

Freebody, P., Luke, A., Gee, J., & Street, B.V. (in press). *Literacy as critical social practice*. London: Falmer.

Gee, J.G. (1996). *Social linguistics and literacies: Idealogy in discourses* (2nd ed.). London: Taylor & Francis.

Gilbert, P. (1988). Stoning the romance: Girls as resistant readers and writers. *Curriculum Perspectives, 8*(2), 13–18.

Gilbert, P., & Taylor, S. (1991). *Fashioning the feminine: Girls, popular culture and schooling*. Sydney, Australia: Allen & Unwin.

Giroux, H.A. (1997). Are Disney movies good for your kids? In. S.R. Steinberg & J.L. Kincheloe (Eds.), *Kinderculture: The corporate construction of childhood* (pp. 53–67). Boulder, CO: Westview.

Goodman, K.S. (1967). Reading: A psycholinguistic guessing game. *Journal of the Reading Specialist, 4*, 126–135.

Goodman, Y.M. (1985). Kidwatching: Observing children in the classroom. In A. Jagger & M.T. Smith-Burke (Eds.), *Observing the language learner* (pp. 9–18). Newark, DE: International Reading Association.

Grace, D.J., & Tobin, J. (1998). Butt jokes and mean-teacher parodies: Video production in the elementary classroom. In D. Buckingham (Ed.), *Teaching popular culture: Beyond radical pedagogy*. London: University College London Press.

Green, B. (1997). Reading with an attitude. In S. Muspratt, A. Luke, & P. Freebody (Eds.), *Constructing critical literacies: Teaching and learning textual practice* (pp. 227–242). Cresskill, NJ: Hampton Press.

144

Green, B. (1998). Learning theory and post critical pedagogy. In D. Buckingham (Ed.), *Teaching popular culture: Beyond radical pedagogy* (pp. 177–197). London: University College London Press.

Hammer, J. (1998, March 23). Catchy kitsch. *Newsweek*, p. 47.

Harper, H. (1996). Reading, identity, and desire: High school girls and feminist avant-garde literature. *Journal of Curriculum Theorizing, 12*(4), 6–13.

Hilton, M. (Ed.). (1996). *Potent fictions: Children's literacy and the challenge of popular culture*. New York: Routledge.

Hinchey, P.H. (1998). *Finding freedom in the classroom: A practical introduction to critical theory*. New York: Peter Lang.

Hodge, B., & Tripp, D. (1986). *Children and television: A semiotic approach*. Cambridge, UK: Polity.

hooks, b. (1994, February). Sexism and misogyny: Who takes the rap? *Z Magazine*, 26–29.

Kloer, P. (1998, April 16). We love to watch. *The Atlanta Journal-Constitution*, p. D1.

Lewis, C. (1997). The social drama of literature discussions in a fifth/sixth-grade classroom. *Research in the Teaching of English, 31*(2), 163–204.

Lewis, C. (1998). Rock 'n' roll and horror stories: Students, teachers, and popular culture. *Journal of Adolescent and Adult Literacy, 42*, 116–120.

Luke, A. (1994). On reading and the sexual division of literacy. *Journal of Curriculum Studies, 26*, 361–381.

Luke, A., & Freebody, P. (1997a). Critical literacy and the question of normativity: An introduction. In S. Muspratt, A. Luke, & P. Freebody (Eds.), *Constructing critical literacies: Teaching and learning textual practice* (pp. 1–18). Cresskill, NJ: Hampton Press.

Luke, A., & Freebody, P. (1997b). Shaping the social practices of reading. In S. Muspratt, A. Luke, & P. Freebody (Eds.), *Constructing critical literacies: Teaching and learning textual practice* (pp. 185–225). Cresskill, NJ: Hampton Press.

Luke, C. (1994). Feminist pedagogy and critical media literacy. *Journal of Communication Inquiry, 18*(2), 30–47.

Luke, C. (1997). Media literacy and cultural studies. In S. Muspratt, A. Luke, & P. Freebody (Eds.), *Constructing critical literacies: Teaching and learning textual practice* (pp. 19–49). Cresskill, NJ: Hampton Press, Inc.

Luke, C. (1998). Pedagogy and authority: Lessons from feminist and cultural studies, postmodernism and feminist pedagogy. In D. Buckingham (Ed.), *Teaching popular culture: Beyond radical pedagogy* (pp. 18–41). London: University College London Press.

Luke, C., & Luke, H. (May, 1997). Techno-textuality: Representation of femininity and sexuality. *Media International Australia, 84*, 46–58.

145

Luke, C., & Roe, K. (1993). Introduction to special issues: Media and popular cultural studies in the classroom. *Australian Journal of Education, 37*(2), 115–118.

Lumby, C. (1997). *Bad girls.* St. Leonards, Australia: Allen & Unwin.

MacGillivray, L., & Martinez, A.M. (1998). Princesses who commit suicide: Primary children writing within and against gender stereotypes. *Journal of Literacy Research, 30,* 53–84.

Marin, R. (1998, March 23). South Park: The rude tube. *Newsweek,* 56–62.

Masterman, L. (1985). *Teaching the media.* London: Comedia.

McLaren, P.L., & Lankshear, C. (1993). Critical literacy and the postmodern turn. In C. Lankshear & P.L. McLaren (Eds.), *Critical literacy: Politics, praxis, and the postmodern* (pp. 379–419). Albany, NY: State University of New York Press.

Morgan, R. (1998). Provocations for a media education in small letters. In D. Buckingham (Ed.), *Teaching popular culture: Beyond radical pedagogy* (pp. 107–131). London: University College London Press.

Morrison, T. (1970). *The bluest eye.* New York: Washington Square Press.

Moss, G. (1993). Children talking horror videos: Reading as a social performance. *Australian Journal of Education, 37*(2), 169–181.

Murdock, G. (1997). Cultural studies at the crossroads. In A. McRobbie (Ed.), *Back to reality? Social experience and cultural studies* (pp. 58–73). Manchester, UK: Manchester University Press.

Neilsen, L. (1998). Playing for real: Performative texts and adolescent literacies. In D.E. Alvermann, K.A. Hinchman, D.W. Moore, S.F. Phelps, & D.R. Waff (Eds.), *Reconceptualizing the literacies in adolescents' lives* (pp. 3–26). Mahwah, NJ: Erlbaum.

O'Brien, D.G. (1998). Multiple literacies in a high-school program for "at risk" adolescents. In D.E. Alvermann, K.A. Hinchman, D.W. Moore, S.F. Phelps, & D.R. Waff (Eds.), *Reconceptualizing the literacies in adolescents' lives* (pp. 27–49). Mahwah, NJ: Erlbaum.

Pompe, C. (1996). "But they're pink!"—"Who cares!": Popular culture in the primary years. In M. Hilton (Ed.), *Potent fictions: Children's literacy and the challenge of popular culture* (pp. 92–125). London: Routledge.

Provenzo, E.F., Jr. (1997). Video games and the emergence of interactive media for children. In S.R. Steinberg & J.L. Kincheloe (Eds.), *Kinderculture: The corporate construction of childhood* (pp. 103–113). Boulder, CO: Westview.

Radway, J. (1984). *Reading the romance: Women, patriarchy and popular literature.* Chapel Hill, NC: University of North Carolina Press.

Richards, C. (1998). Beyond classroom culture. In D. Buckingham (Ed.), *Teaching popular culture: Beyond radical pedagogy* (pp. 132–152). London: University College London Press.

Robinson, M. (1997). *Children reading print and television.* London: Falmer.

Robinson, M. (1998). South Park kicks ass! *INsite, 2*(6), 25–26.

Rosenblatt, L.M. (1938). *Literature as exploration.* New York: Modern Language Association.

Rosenblatt, L.M. (1978). *The reader, the text, the poem: The transactional theory of the literary work.* Carbondale, IL: Southern University Press.

Ruddell, R.B., Ruddell, M.R., & Singer, H. (1994). *Theoretical models and processes of reading* (4th ed.). Newark, DE: International Reading Association.

Sarland, C. (1991). *Young people reading: Culture and response.* Milton Keynes, UK: Open University Press.

Saussure, F. de. (1960). *Course in general linguistics.* London: Peter Owen.

Sholle, D., & Denski, S. (1993). Reading and writing the media: Critical media literacy and postmodernism. In C. Lankshear & P.L. McLaren (Eds.), *Critical literacy: Politics, praxis, and the postmodern* (pp. 297–321). Albany, NY: State University of New York Press.

Smith, F. (1971). *Understanding reading: A psycholinguistic analysis of reading and learning to read.* New York: Holt, Rinehart.

The Spice Girls. (1997). *Spiceworld: The official book of the movie.* New York: Three Rivers Press.

Steinberg, S.R. (1997). The bitch who has everything. In S.R. Steinberg & J.L. Kincheloe (Eds.), *Kinderculture: The corporate construction of childhood* (pp. 207–218). Boulder, CO: Westview.

Tabouret-Keller, A. (1997). Language and identity. In F. Coulmas (Ed.), *The handbook of sociolinguistics* (pp. 315–326). Oxford, UK: Blackwell.

Thigpen, D.E. (1998, April 13). Angst with sugar on it. *Time, 223.*

Urquhart, I. (1996). Popular culture and how boys become men. In M. Hilton (Ed.), *Potent fictions: Children's literacy and the challenge of popular culture* (pp. 150–184). New York: Routledge.

Vinz, R. (1996). Horrorscapes (in)forming adolescent identity and desire. *Journal of Curriculum Theorizing, 12*(4), 14–26.

Vygotsky, L.S. (1962). *Thought and language* (A. Kozalin, Trans.). Cambridge, MA: Massachusetts Institute of Technology Press. (Original work published 1934)

Walkerdine, V. (1990). *Schoolgirl fictions.* London: Verso.

Weaver, D., & Alvermann, D.E. (in press). Critical thinking and discussion. In K. Woods (Ed.), *Promoting literacy in the twenty-first century: A handbook for teachers and administrators in Grades 4–8.* Boston, MA: Allyn & Bacon.

West, C., & Zimmerman, D.H. (1987). Doing gender. *Gender & Society, 1,* 125–151.

Wloszczyna, S. (1998, June 18). "Mulan" breaks the mold. *USA Today,* p. 1D.

Worthy, J. (1998). "On every page someone gets killed!" Book conversations you don't hear in school. *Journal of Adolescent & Adult Literacy, 41,* 508–517.

Author Index

T–U

V

W–Z

Subject Index

Page references followed by *t* or *f* indicate tables or figures, respectively.

G

H

I

J

6549

K–L

M

O

students' feedback, 56–57; teacher's role in lesson, 43; ways to extend the lesson, 57–58
PRODIGY SOFTWARE, 16
PUFF DADDY AND THE FAMILY, 66–68, 71–75, 73*t*, 75*t*
PULP FICTION, 13–14

R

RAP MUSIC, 111
RAY, JIMMY, 16
READINGS. *See* contradictory reading of texts; response of readers
REFLEXIVE POSITIONING, 112
RELEVANCY OF TEXTS, 38–39
"RENEGADE READERS," 140
RESEARCH IMPLICATIONS, 134–138, 141; critical theory's use as framework, 135–136; directions for improving practice, 137–138; objections to critical theory, 136–137
RESPONSES OF READERS, 2–4, 122; audiences' responses, 29–31, 127–134; challenging monolithic view, 109, 129; discourse community membership as factor, 11–21; experiential theories of response, 122; feminist avant-garde literature, 124–126; horror fiction, 36–37, 123–124; variety of readings possible, 35, 109. *See also* contradictory reading of texts; pleasures
ROCK MUSIC. *See* music; specific musical groups or artists

S

SECRET PLEASURES. *See* pleasures
SELF AND OTHER. *See* otherness, notions of
SELF-IDENTITY, 110–111. *See also* identities
SELF-REFLEXIVE APPROACH, 28, 139
SEMIOTICS AND THE INTERPRETATION OF SIGNS, 9–10
SEXISM. *See* entries starting with gender
SOCIAL ASPECTS OF READING, 2
SOFTWARE ADVERTISING, 16–18
SOUTH PARK, 3, 6, 8, 15–16, 44
SPICE GIRLS, 88–92, 91*f*, 95–99, 95*f*, 96*t*–98*t*, 106
STEREOTYPING, 111, 138. *See also* gendered identities; positioning
STINE, R.L., 9, 61. *See also* horror genre
STUDENTS' PLEASURES. See pleasures
SUPERHEROES, USE IN PRIMARY GRADE LESSON, 42–60

T

TARANTINO, QUENTIN, 13–14

TEACHERS: authority role of, 40, 141; flexibility in roles, 39–40, 59, 69; guide role of, 40; honesty in answering class, 101, 106; learner role of, 40, 139; role in leading critical media literacy study, 3–4, 23–29, 32, 38–40, 43, 59, 69, 140–141; views of popular culture, 22–29

TELEVISION: latchkey children and, 7; "Turn Off the TV" initiative, 24; viewing/reading, 132–134. *See also* specific shows by name

TITANIC, 51, 53*f*

U–V

UPPER ELEMENTARY SCHOOL LESSON (MARGARET'S LESSON), 61–84; analysis by students, 74*t*–75*t*; background, 8–9; choice of examples, 63–64; choice of topic, 62–63; designing the lesson, 68–69; student responses, 70*t*, 73*t*; survey of students, 64–66, 65*f*; teacher's role, 69; teaching the lesson, 70–83

VALIDATION OF STUDENTS' POPULAR CULTURE INTERESTS, 31

VIDEO MAGAZINE AIMED AT CHILDREN, 118

VIDEO PRODUCTION ACTIVITY AND PLEASURE, 32

VIOLENCE, 68, 72, 111

W

WALT DISNEY MOVIES AND CHARACTERS, 8, 116–118

"WILD WORDS," READING AND WRITING OF, 124–126

WORLD WIDE WEB. *See* Internet